K N O W
WHAT
YOU
BELIEVE

KNOW
WHAT
YOU
BELIEVE

PAUL E. LITTLE

Revised Edition
including Bible quotations from the
New International Version

While this book is intended for your personal reading pleasure and profit, it is also designed for group
study. A leader's guide is available from your local
bookstore or from the publisher.

VICTOR BOOKS®
A DIVISION OF SCRIPTURE PRESS PUBLICATIONS INC.
USA CANADA ENGLAND

Most Scripture quotations are from the *Holy Bible, New International Version,* © 1973, 1978, 1984, International Bible Society, by permission of Zondervan Bible Publishers. A few quotations are from the *King James Version* (KJV).

38 39 40 Printing/Year 97 96 95

Recommended Dewey Decimal Classification: 291.2
Suggested Subject Headings: RELIGIOUS BELIEF; TRUST IN GOD

Library of Congress Catalog Card Number: 76-105667
ISBN: 0-89693-045-9

CONTENTS

◆

PREFACE

"People Who Don't Believe the Bible Have Never Read It."

Some men write books in an ivory tower, shut off from the world with paper and pen (or computer). The author of this book, my husband, was not one of this kind. Paul wrote his books in the midst of a packed schedule of travel, lecturing, and "eyeball-to-eyeball" conversations with university students. He began talking about his faith while still a student at the University of Pennsylvania and when he graduated, he turned from accounting, his major, to a full-time career of telling the message of Jesus Christ to the student world. He took his message to schools from coast to coast in the United States and on five continents. It seemed his suitcase was incessantly getting either packed or unpacked!

In the course of his relentless schedule, Paul learned to capture his audiences with extraordinary wit. He'd say: "It doesn't matter what you think of Play-Doh, Napoleon, or Richard Nixon. It does matter what you think of Jesus Christ." Or he'd invent graphic illustrations like saying, "The Christian experience is not like a man with a fried egg on his ear who claims the egg gives him peace and joy. Rather, the Christian experience is securely bound to the objective, historical fact of the resurrection of Jesus Christ."

But there was more than wit that kept Paul's books selling widely long after his death. I saw him aim his messages, whether in the university or in the church, for the nontheologian, the person in the classroom or the pew. He was never wishy-washy but could sort out the central biblical truths and express them in lucid simplicity. When he sensed that some non-Christians got hung up on peripheral questions like how churches function or how Christians act, it concerned him. He knew they were missing the life-changing impact that Jesus Christ could bring to their lives. He'd say, "I want to make the message clear. Most people who don't believe the Bible have never read it!"

This need for a clear explanation of what Christians believe hung heavy on Paul's soul until he finally began to write something on paper, and I knew a book was about to be born. He called it *Know What You Believe*. In it he covers questions he'd heard people ask: "Is God a pure mathematical mind, a ball of fire, or a celestial policeman?" And, "Does God first reconcile me and then love me?" And then, "Does God give out little packages of peace, joy, love, etc.?" and many others.

For seventeen years people from all walks of life have read this book. The student, the church member, the non-church member have used it extensively. Now for this new edition, after 24 printings, I have done some minor updating and changed most biblical references to the *New International Version*. It is still entirely Paul's original work. Along with his first two books, *How to Give Away Your Faith* and *Know Why You Believe*, this book has sold hundreds of thousands of copies. Many letters have come to me to tell of God's sovereign work through Paul's writings. I am amazed and deeply grateful to God for the people touched and the lives changed. This excerpt from one of these letters describes more eloquently that I could the power of the Lord Himself revealed in these works:

> My husband and I were having problems getting along. I thought it would do him good to read *Know What You Believe*. But when I began reading it myself I realized I was not a Christian. I knelt down and prayed to the Lord. Now we are both trusting the Lord and our relationship has been completely healed. B.C., Chicago, Illinois.

Marie Little
Park Ridge, Illinois

8

CHAPTER ONE

The Bible

hat is the Bible—this Book that has far and away been the bestseller of all history and has been translated into more languages than any other book?

Bible means "book." But what kind of book is the Bible? Some suggest it is a record of man's religious striving toward and encounters with God—an essentially human book. Until the latter half of the last century, however, the historic Christian church had always seen the Bible as far more than this— namely, as the written Word of God. There was no doctrine on which there was greater unity among Christians. Not until recently have widespread doubts been raised.

The question of the Bible is a crucial one because it involves the whole issue of revelation. How can we know God exists? How can we know about Him, even if He *does* exist? It is clear that our finite minds cannot penetrate His infinity. Job asked, "Can you fathom the mysteries of God? Can you probe the limits of the Almighty?" (Job 11:7) The answer is, only as God takes the initiative in revealing Himself.

God has revealed Himself in several ways. Nature and creation are proofs that God exists and that He is powerful (Rom. 1:19-20). God has revealed Himself through history, particularly in His dealings with Israel and the nations surrounding her.

Such Old Testament expressions as, "Then Manasseh knew that the Lord is God" (2 Chron. 33:13), reflect recognition of God because of His activity in the affairs of men and nations.

God's revelation came to man not only through events themselves, but through the words of the prophets who *interpreted* the events. "The word of the Lord came to me," and, "this is what the Lord says," are recurring phrases throughout the Old Testament (cf. Ezek. 6:1; 7:1; 12:1; Zech. 8:1; Ex. 4:22; 1 Sam. 2:27) of what is called propositional revelation.

God's fullest revelation came in the person of His Son, Jesus Christ. The writer to the Hebrews summarizes it this way: "In the past God spoke to our forefathers through the prophets at many times and in various ways, but in these last days He has spoken to us by His Son" (Heb. 1:1-2).

Written Record Needed

But what about people who were not present and so did not see God's involvement in history or the events surrounding Christ's incarnation, life, death, and resurrection? To reach *all* men, obviously, a written record was needed. God has given this to us in the Bible, through which He has revealed Himself.

The Bible consists of two sections: the Old Testament (or Covenant), consisting of thirty-nine books, and the New Testament (or Covenant), consisting of twenty-seven books. In the Hebrew Bible, the books of the Old Testament are arranged in three divisions—the Law, the Prophets, and the Writings.

In the Septuagint, a translation of the Hebrew Old Testament into Greek made during the third century B.C., the books are arranged according to similarity of subject matter. The Pentateuch (the Law, or five books of Moses) is followed by the historical books. Then come the books of Poetry and Wisdom and, finally, the Prophets. This is the order of the books in most Christian editions of the Bible today. The writing of the Old Testament covered a span of a thousand years.

The twenty-seven New Testament books are in four groups:

the four Gospels, the Acts of the Apostles, twenty-one letters (epistles), and the Revelation. These books were written within the span of a century. The earliest documents were the first letters of Paul, which, along with perhaps the letter of James, were written between A.D. 48 and 60, and the Gospels and other books between A.D. 60 and 100.

How did the Bible come to be written? Two clear statements from the New Testament answer this question: "Understand that no prophecy of Scripture came about by the prophet's own interpretation. For prophecy never had its origin in the will of man, but men spoke from God as they were carried along by the Holy Spirit" (2 Peter 1:20-21); "All Scripture is God-breathed and is useful for teaching, rebuking, correcting and training in righteousness" (2 Tim. 3:16).

Given by Inspiration

The Bible originated in the mind of God, not in the mind of man. It was given to man by *inspiration.* It is important to understand this term because its biblical meaning is different from that which we often give it in everyday language. The Bible is not inspired as the writings of a great novelist are inspired, or as Bach's music was inspired. Inspiration, in the biblical sense, means that God so superintended the writers of Scripture that they wrote what He wanted them to write and were kept from error in so doing. The word *inspired* (2 Tim. 3:16) actually means "outbreathed" (by God). Inspiration applies to the end result—the Scripture itself—as well as to the men whom God used to write the Scripture.

This does not mean that the human writers of Scripture were practically machines through whom God dictated. Nor does it mean that they were human typewriters whom God punched. On the contrary, their full personalities entered into their writings. Their individual writing styles are evident, for instance. Their backgrounds also are often apparent in what they wrote. But though their human capacities came into play, they were superintended and borne along in a unique way by the Holy Spirit. Because of this, the Bible is called "the Word of God"

11

(see such passages as Mark 7:13 and Hebrews 4:12).

It is clear that some material in the Bible came directly from God; it could not otherwise have been known by the human mind. Genesis 1–2 is an example of this sort of material, which must have been made known to Moses supernaturally. In other cases, men recorded events which they themselves witnessed; e.g., John wrote about his approach, with Peter, to the empty tomb on the first Easter morning (John 20:3-10). Some writers used records that were already in existence, as Luke did in writing his Gospel (Luke 1:1-4). In other instances, God put into men's mouths the very words they should speak, or told them what to write: "This is the word that came to Jeremiah from the Lord: 'This is what the Lord, the God of Israel, says: "Write in a book all the words I have spoken to you" ' " (Jer. 30:1-2).

To say that the Scripture is inspired is not to say that all of the attitudes and ideas mentioned in the Bible are directly from God. Some of the record includes the words of evil and foolish men and even of Satan himself. Such parts are not revelation as such, nor are they the words of God, yet they are recorded in Scripture by God's intention and inspiration.

In the Book of Job, for instance, the words of Jehovah, the words of Satan, the speeches of Job's three friends, and the words of Job himself are given. All are not equally authoritative, but inspiration guarantees that what each one said was accurately recorded.

It is a striking fact that however the words came to be recorded, all Scripture is viewed by the writers as from God. Paul speaks of Scripture as "the very words of God" (Rom. 3:2). Most significant of all, the apostles and our Lord Himself quoted the Old Testament—not merely as the counsel of a particular patriarch or prophet, but as the counsel of *God* given through the writers: "You spoke by the Holy Spirit through the mouth of your servant, our father David" (Acts 4:24-25).

Other passages speak of God as if *He* were the Scriptures. For example: "For the Scripture says to Pharaoh: 'I raised you up for this very purpose, that I might display My power in you and that My name might be proclaimed in all the earth' "

(Rom. 9:17; cf. Ex. 9:16). Benjamin Warfield pointed out that these instances of the Scriptures being spoken of as if they were God, and of God being spoken of as if He were the Scriptures, could only result from a habitual identification of the text of Scripture with God speaking. It became natural to use the terms "Scripture says," and "God says," synonymously. In other words, "Scripture" and the speaking of God were seen as identical.[1]

Extent of Inspiration

The question of the extent of inspiration is frequently raised and is an important issue today. The terms *plenary* and *verbal* inspiration are used. *Plenary* means "full." When used in connection with inspiration, it means that all of Scripture is inspired—not merely some parts. Some take the position that the only inspired (and therefore inerrant) parts of the Bible are those having to do with spiritual issues and salvation. These people maintain that to apply the claim of inspiration (and consequently inerrancy or trustworthiness) to matters involving human history or the physical world (science) is to encounter insuperable barriers.

Some scholars hold that the Bible "contains" the Word of God rather than *is* the Word of God. This view, however, confronts us with a serious problem. How can we know what parts of the Bible are trustworthy and what parts are not? How do we know which aspects have to do entirely with salvation and which are "only" matters of history? Often the two—salvation and history—are inextricably intertwined. For instance, if the Cross and the Resurrection are not historical events, of what value are they in salvation?

Moreover, if the Bible's references to the physical world and to history are not trustworthy, on what basis can we be sure that those portions dealing with salvation are trustworthy? If we are going to pick and choose the parts of the Bible we can believe, we must depend on personal subjective judgment. On matters involving eternal destiny, this is a shaky basis on which to proceed.

There have been three bases of religious authority. The first is tradition, or the authority of the church, to which Roman Catholics have adhered. The second is human reason, which liberal thinkers have adopted. The third is the Bible itself, which evangelicals have always recognized as authoritative. To take this third position is not to deny the value of tradition and of human reason, but to submit them, in case of conflict, to the authority of Scripture.

Evangelicals do not deny that there are problems in reconciling some statements of Scripture with what historical data we possess. But the evidence of modern archeology has, with few exceptions, confirmed the Bible record, so it would not seem unreasonable to postpone judgment on the questions still in doubt.

The term *verbal inspiration* indicates that inspiration extends to the *words* of the Bible themselves, not only to the ideas. We have already seen that God did not "dictate" the Scripture mechanically, but guided and superintended the writers within the framework of their own personalities and backgrounds. This guidance would of necessity include their choice of words, since thoughts are composed of words, much as a bar of music consists of individual notes. To alter the notes alters the music. Verbal inspiration holds that God, by His Spirit, has guaranteed the authenticity and reliability of the very words that were written, without depriving the writers of their individuality. A Christian who has a high view of inspiration is, of all people, sincerely interested in using modern tools in textual study to determine the original text.

The inspiration of which the Scripture speaks applies only to the text *as originally produced by the writers.* There have been some errors in copying, though they are fewer and less significant than one would think.

We have observed that the Bible *is* the Word of God; it does not merely *contain* the Word of God, as many believe. Others say the Bible *becomes* the Word of God to an individual when the person has an "existential encounter" with God in his reading of Scripture—when the truth of a passage makes a powerful and indelible impression on him. Those who hold this position are often in strong reaction to "dead" orthodoxy—to the profession of evangelical beliefs unaccompanied by evidence of the believer's having been changed by God's power.

Holy Spirit Illuminates

Scripture must be illumined in the heart of an individual by the Holy Spirit before it becomes meaningful to him. Before the coming of the Spirit at Pentecost, the Father and the Son had revealed divine truth. When Peter answered our Lord's climactic question, "Who do you say I am?" with, "You are the Christ, the Son of the living God," Jesus said, "Blessed are you, Simon son of Jonah, for this was not revealed to you by man, but by My *Father* in heaven" (Matt. 16:15-17, italics added). When Jesus was talking to the two disciples on the road to Emmaus after His resurrection, *He* "explained to them what was said in all the Scriptures concerning Himself." As He sat with them, "their eyes were opened and they recognized Him" (Luke 24:27, 31). "Then *He* opened their minds so they could understand the Scriptures" (24:45, italics added). In telling the disciples about His going away, He said, "But when He, the Spirit of Truth, comes, He will guide you into all truth" (John 16:13).

God reveals by the Spirit what He has prepared for those who love Him (1 Cor. 2:9-10). The illuminating work of the Spirit of God is necessary if we are to know *anything* about God. What the Holy Spirit illumines is "the sword of the Spirit, which is the Word of God" (Eph. 6:17). It does not *become* the Word of God; it *is* the Word of God.

A television set, sitting in the corner but not turned on, is still a television set. I won't get any images or sound until I turn it on, but it *is* a television set, whether turned on or not. It doesn't *become* a television set when turned on.

So too the Scripture *is* the Word of God, whether anybody ever responds to it or not. The Holy Spirit must illumine Scripture in a person's heart before it becomes *meaningful,* but what He illumines *is* the Word of God, not something less. It doesn't *become* something it wasn't before.

Having seen that the Bible *is* the Word of God, we must now consider the principles of interpreting and understanding it. Considerable confusion has resulted because people have oversimplified the kinds of biblical interpretation as either "literal" or "figurative." Those who take the Bible literally are made to look foolish by their apparent denial of any use of figures of speech in the Bible. Those, on the other hand, who take it figuratively often appear to be capricious in evading the clear meaning of statements they do not want to accept.

The fact is that some parts of the Bible are to be taken literally and other parts figuratively.

The key question is, what did the writer intend his readers to understand? We must ask to whom the passage was written. Is the promise or command, for instance, one that has universal application or one that has limited reference? Often there are primary and secondary applications. A primary application has to do with the person or people directly addressed. A secondary application relates a scriptural principle to those to whom the passage is not applied directly.

It is important to consider the context in which a Bible statement is made. What is the primary teaching of the passage? Statements must not be lifted out of context in such a way as to cause misunderstanding. A skeptic once triumphantly asserted, "The Bible says, 'There is no God.' " He was considerably deflated when reminded of the context: "The fool says in his heart, 'There is no God' " (Ps. 14:1).

Literal or Figurative?

It is important to decide accurately if a statement is literal or figurative. The Bible uses such literary forms as poetry, allegory, and parable. Though there are passages on which there is strong difference of opinion, it is usually no more difficult to distinguish between figurative and literal statements in the Bible than in a daily newspaper. The statement "Two people were killed in an accident on Main Street" is obviously literal. "He shot home from third in the last half of the ninth with the winning run under his arm, and the crowd went mad" is readily recognized as figurative language. A player does not "shoot" home or carry runs under his arm. And the fans in the bleachers, though they may get excited, do not become insane.

A final word about Bible study. Simply using a good dictionary to investigate the full meaning of the words of Scripture will reveal surprising riches. Try it! And consult several translations.

It has been said that the Scripture is its own best commentary. Often a verse or a passage becomes clear when studied in the light of other Bible statements on the same subject. Though humanly the Bible has many writers, in the final analysis there was only one Author—God Himself. As we compare Scripture with Scripture, we are guarded against becoming unbalanced in our views. We need to study individual books and we also need to trace themes through the whole Bible. This is the difference between biblical theology and systematic theology. One scholar compares biblical theology to "the profusion of nature in which the various plants and flowers are scattered with a bountiful hand in 'ordered disorder.' " He compares systematic theology to a botanical garden "where plants and flowers are gathered and arranged according to species."[2] Both kinds of arrangements are useful; both have their place in a study of botany. Both kinds of Bible study are useful too.

The Canon of Scripture

A separate question from that of inspiration is that of the canon, i.e., *which* writings, or books, are recognized as *inspired?* It is important to realize that a book did not become inspired by being included in the canon. Inclusion in the canon was merely recognition of the authority the book already possessed.

We do not know exactly when the Old Testament canon was completed. The Old Testament itself says that collections of "authorized" books were put in the sacred buildings—the tabernacle and then the temple. Hilkiah rediscovered the Book of the Law there (2 Kings 22). The Jews recognized as their Scriptures certain books that recorded Jehovah's dealings with Israel.

In our Lord's time, the Old Testament was viewed as a completed collection. He and the apostles referred to this collection as "the Scripture." Most of the books of the Old Testament are quoted in the New Testament, always as authoritative.

In tracing the canonicity of a particular book—that is, its recognition as one of the inspired writings—we must keep three questions in mind: (1) Is it mentioned by the early church fathers in the Christian literature of the first centuries of our era? (2) What attitude do these early writers take toward the inspiration of the book? (3) Do they regard it as part of a canon, or list of books recognized as inspired?

The definition of the canon was important in the early church because claims were being advanced for many writings which were patently spurious, and because heretics were attacking the validity of the genuine Scriptures. The canon, as we know it today, became fixed when Athanasius (A.D. 297-373), patriarch of Alexandria and considered the father of orthodoxy, listed the books of the New Testament in his thirty-ninth Paschal Letter (A.D. 367).

The canon of the New Testament was also confirmed at a church council held in Carthage in A.D. 397. The council used three criteria in recognizing canonicity. First, was a book apostolic in origin? The Gospels of Mark and Luke were accepted, for example, because they were recognized as the work of close associates of the apostles. Second, was the book used and recognized by the churches? Third, did the book teach sound doctrine?[3]

It is on these bases that the orthodox Protestant church today does not receive as canonical the twelve books of the Apocrypha (1—2 Maccabees, 1—2 Esdras, Tobit, Judith, Wisdom of Solomon, Ecclesiasticus, Baruch, Song of the Three Holy Children, Susanna, Bel and the Dragon, and the Prayer of Manasses), which the Roman Catholic church accepts. The Jews never recognized these books as part of their Old Testament.

To accept the Bible as the Word of God today is not fashionable. Some, even within the professing church, deny its reliability. Generally, attacks on Scripture follow certain lines. Perhaps the foremost is that of contending that the Bible is incompatible with twentieth-century science. Many conflicts are said to exist between scientific facts and statements in the Bible. There are, admittedly, some problems. But the following considerations usually bridge what on first sight may seem a yawning chasm.

Understanding the Bible

First, the Bible speaks in *phenomenological* language—that is, it describes things *as they appear to be* rather than in precise scientific terms. To say the sun rises in the east is a phenomenological statement. Technically, we know the sun does not really "rise," but even the *Naval Almanac* uses the term *sunrise*, and we would not charge the almanac with error. The Bible has been understandable in all cultures and throughout history because of the phenomenological way it actually describes things. It does not at all claim to be a science textbook, but where it touches scientific matters, it does not give misinformation.

Second, when Bible information is incomplete, it is not necessarily incorrect. Science is always building on previous knowledge. Advancement on incomplete theories does not mean the theories were incorrect.

Third, we must always guard against making the Bible say things which, on closer examination, it really doesn't say. And it is most important to determine whether, in a given instance, the Bible is speaking figuratively or literally.

Fourth, we must carefully investigate to see whether the supposed conflict is between biblical teaching and scientific facts or simply between an *interpretation* of Scripture and an *interpretation* of the facts. Often an interpretation at variance with biblical truth is more philosophic than scientific.

Fifth, it would be foolish to "freeze" the points of conflict and assume the Bible wrong. The Bible has not changed in 2,000 years, but science admittedly is a moving train. To have reconciled the Bible to scientific views current a century ago would have been to make Scripture obsolete today! Far better to *admit* an apparent conflict and await the development of additional evidence.

That there is no basic conflict between science and Scripture is suggested by the fact that modern science was born and developed largely by earnest Christians. Believing in a personal God as Creator, they were convinced that the universe was orderly and therefore capable of meaningful investigation. In scientific research, they felt they were thinking God's thoughts after Him. There can be no ultimate conflict between truth of biblical revelation and that discovered by science, for all truth is from God and is therefore consistent. In our day, when some 90 percent of all scientists who have ever lived are alive, many outstanding scientists are also earnest Christians.

Dating Problems Explained

In another line of attack it is contended that the Bible is not reliable historically and that there are "internal" contradictions in parallel accounts of the same event. Some apparent numerical errors may be due to mistakes in transmission of the text over many years. Recent archaeological discoveries, however, show that the ancients' system of dating explains many numerical problems. If one king, for example, ended his rule and another began ruling in a given calendar year, *both* were given credit for ruling the entire year. Also, it is important to remember that the biblical writers often used round figures which, though not precise, are at the same time not incorrect.

Admittedly we do not presently have complete explanations for all seeming Bible discrepancies. But it would be unscientific, in light of modern archaeological discoveries, to adopt the prevalent assumption that the Bible is wrong until proven right, rather than the reverse. An ever increasing number of excavations from Egypt to Babylonia have told us more clearly the life and history of Bible lands. Thousands of records etched in stone tablets dating back to 3,000 years before Christ have been quarried and subsequently translated. Alan R. Millard, senior lecturer at the University of Liverpool, states: "All of these discoveries have increased our knowledge of the world in which the Bible was written, so they enable its distinctive message to stand out more boldly. Rightly interpreted, the Bible and archaeology can only enrich each other."[4]

We do not "prove" the Bible by archaeology. The Holy Spirit confirms in our hearts the conviction that the Bible is the Word of God.

We can with confidence affirm with the hymn writer:

The Bible stands like a rock undaunted
  'Mid the raging storms of time;
Its pages burn with the truth eternal,
  And they glow with a light sublime.
The Bible stands though the hills may tumble;
  It will firmly stand when the earth shall crumble;
I will plant my feet on its firm foundation,
  For the Bible stands!

—Haldor Lillenas

"Your Word, O Lord, is eternal; it stands in the heavens" (Ps. 119:89).

CHAPTER TWO

God

hat we believe about God," said the late A.W. Tozer, "is the most important thing about us." Our belief or lack of it inevitably translates itself into our actions and attitudes.

It is interesting to reconstruct the God Joseph believed in from his reactions to his traitorous brothers and his unjust imprisonment. And consider Moses, who, because of the God he trusted, "endured, as seeing Him who is invisible" (Heb. 11:27). He gave up the king's palace for the desert and God's people. Significantly, faith, in Hebrews 11, is illustrated by what people *did* rather than what they *said* or professed.

The word *God* is one of the most widely used terms in our language; yet it is nebulous and undefined in most minds. Some people think of God as "a pure mathematical mind," as did Einstein. Others see Him as a shadowy superhuman person or force. Still others see God as a ball of fire to which we, as sparks of life, will ultimately be reunited. A few think of Him as a sentimental grandfather of the sky and others regard Him as a great celestial policeman.

Increasing godlessness causes some people to urge us to agree simply to use the word *God* without even trying to define it lest we breed division. It is obvious, however, that if God *is*, His existence and His nature do not depend on what anyone thinks about Him. To conceive of God as a stone idol or as a mystical idea does not *make* Him either. If I am interested in *reality*, I must know what God is *really* like. This I cannot know apart from His revealing Himself to me. How God has done this is summed up by the writer to the Hebrews, as previously mentioned: "In the past God spoke to our forefathers through the prophets at many times and in various ways, but in these last days He has spoken to us by His Son" (Heb. 1:1-2).

Because God has spoken and has revealed Himself, we no longer have the need or the option of conjuring up ideas and images of God by our own imaginations. Our personal concept of God—when we pray, for instance—is *worthless* unless it coincides with His revelation of Himself.

God's "Natural" Attributes

The terms that describe the nature of God—love, holiness, sovereignty, etc.—are known as His attributes. They are classified as "natural" attributes and "moral" attributes. Let's think first about God's "natural" attributes, as revealed by His self-disclosure in Scripture.

First, God is separate from His creation. He is *transcendent*—above and beyond His creation, the heavens and the earth. He is not a slave to the natural law He authored, but is independent of it and above it. He can override it at will—though normally He does not interfere with it. He is exalted and eternal, the world's Creator, Sovereign, and Judge.

But God is *immanent* as well as transcendent. By this we mean that His presence and power pervade His entire creation. He does not stand apart from the world, a mere spectator of the things He has made.

The prophet spoke of God's *transcendence* when he wrote of "the high and lofty One . . . who lives forever, whose name is holy [set apart]," and of His *immanence* when he spoke of Him as the One who dwells "with him who is contrite and lowly in spirit" (Isa. 57:15).

God is not so totally transcendent that He set the universe in motion and then left it, as deists would have us believe. Nor is He so immanent that He is indistinguishable from the universe. Pantheism holds that God is all and that all is God. But that means you and I would be part of God, which ultimately means that God sins when we sin. If all is God, and everything else is illusion, as some hold, then what could exist to *have* the illusion? Does God have illusions?

One who sees God in nature is not necessarily a pantheist. The Bible itself tells us that the universe which God has made speaks to us of His eternal power (*omnipotence*) and deity (cf. Rom. 1:19-20). The Rocky Mountains, Niagara Falls, the starry hosts of heaven, the ocean's vastness—all remind us that God made them and is sovereign over them.

The prophet observed, "Ah, Sovereign Lord, You have made the heavens and the earth by Your great power. . . . Nothing is too hard for You" (Jer. 32:17). The Angel Gabriel assured Mary, after informing her of her privilege of bearing the Son of God as a virgin, "For nothing is impossible with God" (Luke 1:37).

The omnipotence of God is limited by His moral character. For example, though "nothing is impossible with God," "it is impossible for God to lie" (Heb. 6:18). His omnipotence applies to inherent possibilities, not inherent impossibilities. Someone has asked, "Is it possible for God to make anything too heavy for Himself to lift? If not, can we say He is omnipotent?" Nonsense is still nonsense, as C.S. Lewis says, whether we are talking about something else or about God.

God's Eternity

God is *eternal*—that is, He never had a beginning and will never have an end. As observed earlier, He is the "One . . . who lives forever" (Isa. 57:15). "The eternal God is your refuge" (Deut. 33:27). From everlasting to everlasting, He is God (cf. Ps. 90:2). The answer to the question, "Who created God?" is, "No one and nothing," because God is completely self-existent. There was never a time when He did not exist.

God is *infinite*. By this we mean that He is not limited by or confined to the universe. He is entirely independent of finite (measurable) things and beings. There have been times when God has put limitations on Himself, as when He appeared to Old Testament believers in the form of an angel or a man (e.g., Gen. 18:1) and when He became incarnate in the person of Jesus Christ. He imposed such limitation on Himself in order to bless His creatures, not because He *had* to.[1]

It has been pointed out that our minds cannot adequately conceive of an *infinite* quantity of anything—space, power, potatoes. Such a concept baffles and frustrates us. We *can*, however, imagine a being—God—who is infinite in the sense that He has no limitations. God's infinite holiness does not mean that He has a boundless *amount* of holiness—for holiness cannot be measured in this way. Rather, it means that His holiness has no limitations and no defeats. The same may be said for each of His other attributes.

God's infinity is also a matter of "boundless activity"—that is, His power (omnipotence) is at work in and in control of everything, anywhere, that exists.[2]

God is *unchangeable*. He "does not change like shifting shadows" (James 1:17). It is important that we not think of God in terms of human personality, which is ordinarily volatile and unsteady. God's love is steadfast and constant, and is not subject to the ebbs and flows of human love. His wrath is a fixed attitude toward sin and is not like our fits of temper when something displeases us.

A man who walks east into a strong east wind, and then turns around and walks west, would say, "The wind *was* on my face, but *now* it is on my back." But there would have been no change in the wind. His *direction* was what changed, and this change brought him into a new relationship with the wind. God never changes, and when He *seems* to be different it is because *we* have changed and in so doing have come into a different relationship toward Him.

When God "Repents"

The Bible speaks of God as *repenting* (changing His mind). The term describes what *seems* to us to have happened. As an instance, God threatened to destroy the ancient city of Nineveh, but after Jonah had preached there the people turned to God for forgiveness and He is said to have repented (Jonah 3:10) of His plan to destroy them. Actually, the Ninevites had turned from rebellion to repentance, and so they came under God's mercy and forgiveness instead of His wrath. God Himself had not changed.

God is *omnipresent*, which means He is fully present everywhere. He is not like a substance spread out in a thin layer all over the earth—*all* of Him is in Chicago, in Calcutta, in Cairo, and in Caracas, at one and the same time.

God is *omniscient*—that is, He knows everything, including our own thoughts. "You know when I sit and when I rise; You perceive my thoughts from afar" (Ps. 139:2), David wrote about God, and the Apostle John wrote of our Lord that "He did not need man's testimony about man, for He knew what was in a man" (John 2:25). Moreover, He declares, "I make known the end from the beginning" (Isa. 46:10); nothing surprises Him.

Jesus declared that "God is spirit, and His worshipers must worship Him in spirit and in truth" (John 4:24). God does not have a physical body. When we speak of the "hand of God" or the "nostrils of God" we are using *anthropomorphisms*—human expressions—to describe God, though we know they are not *literally* true.

We have saved for last the fact about God which, among His "natural" attributes, is of the greatest importance. God is all-powerful, all-wise, infinite and eternal, and changeless, and we are not to think of Him as an impersonal force behind the universe. God is *personal*—that is, He is a Person. He has the elements of personality—intellect, feelings, and will. He is self-determining—as, within our limitations, we also are. He does according to His own purpose and will.

We know this of God because He created man in His own image and after His own likeness (Gen. 1:26). Since *we* are persons, God cannot possibly be something less than a person. What is created cannot be of a higher order than its Creator.

Because God is personal, we know that His sovereign will is

not akin to the blind fate ("Kismet") of Islam's Allah. It is, rather, the loving purpose of a Heavenly Father to whom His children are precious. And because God is a Person and we are persons, communication between Him and us is possible.

God's "Moral" Attributes

God's other qualities are called His "moral" attributes. It is not enough to know merely that God exists; it is desperately important to know about His moral nature. Suppose we believe that God exists, but think of Him as being like Adolf Hitler. What a horrible truth to contemplate, and what a heinous existence we would have!

Holiness is perhaps the most comprehensive of all of God's attributes. "It is a term for the moral excellence of God and His freedom from all limitation in His moral perfection. 'Thou art of purer eyes than to behold evil' (Hab. 1:13, KJV)."[3] In this exalted sense, only God is holy. He is therefore the standard of ethical purity by which His creatures must measure themselves.

"Since holiness embraces every distinctive attribute of the Godhead, it may be defined as the outshining of all that God is. As the sun's rays, combining all the colors of the spectrum, come together in the sun's shining and blend into light, so in His self-manifestation all the attributes of God come together and blend into holiness. Holiness has, for that reason, been called 'an attribute of attributes'—that which lends unity to all the attributes of God. To conceive of God's being and character as merely a [collection] of abstract perfectness is to deprive God of all reality."[4] Holiness is the sum total of the perfections of the God of the Bible.

All the attributes of God are in perfect harmony and are in no way antagonistic to each other. God's love and mercy are not opposed to, or exercised at the expense of, His righteousness and holiness. Sometimes it is wrongly suggested that the God of the Old Testament is a God of wrath and anger, but that the New Testament portrays God in Christ as love and gentleness. The implication is sometimes drawn that these are two different Gods. This, of course, is completely false. The

God of the Old Testament, who repeatedly had mercy on the Israelites after they repented, is the same God who wept over Jerusalem because her people killed the prophets and would not turn to the Lord. The Jesus who spoke frequently of hell and eternal judgment is the same God who moved in judgment on Jerusalem in 586 B.C., and on the pagan King Belshazzar some years later.

Our Triune God

At the heart of the Christian view of God is the concept of the *Trinity*. Rather than being "excess baggage," as the late Episcopal Bishop James A. Pike called it, this truth is central to an understanding of biblical revelation and the Christian Gospel. Departure from the doctrine of the Trinity has been and is one of the major sources of heresy in the Christian church.

The term *Trinity* does not occur anywhere in the Bible, but this does not mean that the idea is a later development or one that is a product of philosophic speculation rather than divine revelation.

The Trinity is a difficult concept, not fully susceptible to human explanation, because it involves categories which our finite mental powers cannot grasp. Anyone who has ever tried to explain the Trinity to an unbeliever will agree that it could hardly be a human invention. It is a teaching which God Himself has revealed to us.

The doctrine is that "God is one in His essential being, but that the 'divine essence' exists in three modes or forms, each constituting a Person, yet in such a way that the divine essence is wholly in each Person."[5] God is one Being, but He exists in three Persons.

The first Old Testament clue concerning the Trinity comes in the story of Creation. God (Elohim) created by means of the Word and the Spirit (Gen. 1:1-3). These immortal words were read by Commander Frank Borman in Apollo 8 as the spacecraft circled the moon: "In the beginning God created the heaven and the earth. And the earth was without form, and void, and darkness was upon the face of the deep. And the

Spirit of God moved upon the face of the waters. And God said, 'Let there be light, and there was light' " (KJV).

R.A. Finlayson states: "Here we are introduced . . . to the Word as a personal creative power, and to the Spirit as the bringer of life and order to the creation. There is revealed thus early a threefold center of activity. God, as Creator, thought out the Universe, expressed His thought in a Word, and made His Spirit its animating principle."[6]

Some believe that when God (Elohim) said, "Let Us make man in Our image" (Gen. 1:26), the plural forms used (Elohim, us, our) are to be understood as a revelation of the Trinity by God to man, and that man's awareness of this truth was later lost through the Fall.

Other indications of the Trinity are to be found in Genesis 48:15-16; Exodus 31:3; Numbers 11:25; Judges 3:10; Proverbs 8:22-31 (the Word is here personified as Wisdom); and Isaiah 11:2; 42:1; 61:1. In these passages, the Spirit is clearly the source of blessing, power, and strength.

The Bible's emphasis throughout, however, is on the fact that God is *one.* "Hear, O Israel: The Lord our God, the Lord is one" (Deut. 6:4). This truth was in sharp contrast to the rampant polytheism that surrounded the nation of Israel in Bible times. We must not allow the scriptural truth of the Trinity to deprive us of the equally important teaching that there is only *one* God.

It is both interesting and significant that in the New Testament, where the distinctness of the persons of the Godhead is clearer, the disciples were taught by our Lord to baptize in *the name* (singular) of the Father and of the Son and of the Holy Spirit (Matt. 28:19).

John the Baptist spoke of the coming baptism of the (Holy) Spirit, of which his own water baptism was a symbol. When John baptized Him, Jesus saw "heaven being torn open, and the Spirit descending upon Him like a dove. And a voice came from heaven: 'You are My Son, whom I love; with You I am well pleased' " (Mark 1:10-11). This was a clear manifestation of the Trinity, all three Persons of the Godhead being referred to.

Earlier, at the birth of Jesus, all three Persons of the God-head are also mentioned. The angel told Mary that her child would be the *Son* of *God* conceived by the *Holy Spirit* (Luke 1:35).

Jesus explicitly spoke of the Father and the Spirit as being distinct Persons from Himself (John 14–16).

Salvation itself portrays the work of the Triune God. The Father sent the Son to accomplish the work of redemption. The Son sent the Spirit to bring conviction and to apply to men what Christ had accomplished.

The apostolic benediction, "The grace of the Lord Jesus Christ, and the love of God, and the fellowship of the Holy Spirit be with you all" (2 Cor. 13:14), is another instance of apostolic teaching on the Trinity.

Each person of the Trinity is fully God. Paul wrote of "God our Father" (Rom. 1:7), and spoke of Christ as the Son He loves. . . the image of the invisible God" (Col. 1:13, 15) and as "God our Saviour" (Titus 3:4).

The deity of the Holy Spirit is also clear. Peter told Ananias that in lying to the Holy Spirit, he had "not lied unto men but to God" (Acts 5:3-4).

A Semantic Problem

Part of the problem of understanding the Trinity is the inade-quacy of human words to express divine reality. For instance, we speak of the "Persons" in the Godhead. We use this term because it describes a being who has intellect, emotion, and will. We can understand this. But we must be careful in apply-ing such terms to God. Finlayson comments:

> In most [cases] the doctrine is stated by saying that God is one in His essential being, but that in this being there are three Persons, yet so as not to form separate and distinct individuals. They are three modes or forms in which the divine essence exists. "Person" is, however, an imperfect expression of the truth, inasmuch as the term denotes to us a *separate* rational and moral individual. But in the

being of God there are not three *individuals,* but only three *personal self distinctions* within the one divine essence.

Then again, personality in man implies independence of will, actions, and feelings, leading to behavior peculiar to the [individual]. This cannot be thought of in connection with the Trinity: each Person is self-conscious and self-directing, yet never acts independently or in opposition [to the others]. When we say that God is a Unity, we mean that though [He] is in Himself a threefold center of life, His life is not split into three. He is one in essence, in personality, and in will. When we say that God is a Trinity in Unity, we mean that there is unity in diversity, and that diversity manifests itself in Persons, in characteristics, and in operations.[7]

Just as the word *person* is not exact when applied to the Godhead, but is the best approximation available, so it is with the word *substance.* The Trinity was spoken of in the early church as "three Persons in one Substance." But here, according to T.C. Hammond, "substance is, of course, immaterial; it must not be thought of either as a common spiritual 'stuff' or 'material' out of which three Beings of the same divine nature are produced (as we talk of silver as the *substance* from which coins [were] made). The divine essence is not *divided* into three: it is fully present in each of the Persons. 'Substance' thus relates to the one Being who is God, rather than to the nature or being of that God."[8]

It is also important to understand the relationships of the Persons of the Trinity. The Son and the Spirit are said to be "subordinate" to the Father, but this does not mean they are inferior. Their subordination has been called a matter of relationship, but not of nature.

"The Father, as the fount of Deity, is first" writes Finlayson. "He is said to *originate.* The Son, eternally begotten of the Father, is second. He is said to *reveal.* The Spirit, eternally proceeding from the Father and the Son, is third. He is said to *execute.* . . . Thus we can say that Creation is from the Father, through the Son, by the Holy Spirit."[9]

The Spirit of God is said to proceed from the Son as well as from the Father. The Father is the One by whom the Son is begotten and from whom the Spirit proceeds.

Two Major Heresies

There have been two major heretical distortions of the Trinity, and they exist at present. One is an attempt to get away from any implication that there are three separate and distinct Persons in the Godhead. Originating with a man named Sabellius in the third century, this error claims that Father, Son, and Holy Spirit are merely different manifestations of the one God which He assumes temporarily to achieve His purposes. At times God appears as Father, at times as Son, and at times as the Holy Spirit, say the Sabellians.

The other emphasis was originated by Arius (about A.D. 325). Though Arius emphasized the unity of God, he so stressed the Persons of the Trinity that he ended up by dividing the substance of the Godhead. "This resulted chiefly from his definition of the Son and the Holy Spirit as being lesser, subordinate Beings whom the Father willed into existence for the purpose of acting as His agents in His dealings with the world and men" according to Hammond. In effect, Arius reduced our Lord (and the Spirit) below the level of strict Deity."[10] Arius would admit (Christ's) deity in a secondary sense, but denied His *eternal* Sonship. He admitted that Christ existed before the foundation of the world, but denied that He was coeternal with the Father. The disciples of Arius, by teaching that the Spirit was brought into existence by the Son, reduced Him to a lesser form of Deity.

In more recent times, some movements, such as Unitarianism, Russellism (Jehovah's Witnesses), and Mormonism assign our Lord and the Holy Spirit a nature and position below that of true Deity. Hammond comments that "This is one of the most important battlegrounds in the history of the church, and no true Christian should for one moment tolerate any description of our Master other than that which assigns to Him the fullest Deity, coequal and coeternal with the Father."[11]

It is also important that we know about God's providence and will if our knowledge of God is to be accurate. He is not only the Creator of the universe—He is also its Sustainer in the physical sense, and is the moral Governor of the intelligent beings He has created. The sweep of God's providence and sovereignty are complete and comprehensive. "The Lord does whatever pleases Him, in the heavens and on the earth, in the seas and all their depths" (Ps. 135:6). This truth is echoed in the New Testament: "They [the rulers] did what Your power and will had decided beforehand should happen" (Acts 4:28). God is the One in whom "all things hold together" (cf. Col. 1:17). He is the One "who works out everything in conformity with the purpose of His will" (Eph. 1:11).

God's Decrees

God's control of the universe is often spoken of in terms of His *decrees.* Someone has defined the decrees of God as "that eternal plan by which God makes sure that all the events of the universe—past, present, and future—take place." To our finite, limited minds there appear to be a great many events, but with God there is no time, and everything happens in one eternal moment. This is why we say God knows the end from the beginning.

A distinction is sometimes made between the absolute *decrees* of God, which determine what happens, and His *purposes* for His creatures—that is, His revelation to them of their duties. God's decrees are always accomplished, but men frequently ignore and disobey His purposes for them.

Another distinction is made between the *directive* will and the *permissive* will of God. His directive will is what He brings to pass; His permissive will is what He allows to take place. God *permitted,* but did not *direct,* the entrance of sin into the world. But whether actively (by decree) or passively (by permission), God is sovereign over all that happens. He is *free* in that He is under no other influence or power of anything or anyone but Himself. "Who has understood the mind of the

Lord, or instructed Him as His counselor?" (Isa. 40:13) He is *sovereign*—He has power to bring His purposes to pass.

What about Free Will?

The question of God's sovereignty and its relation to human freedom troubles many people. If God directs everything, how can man be a free agent and therefore morally responsible? If God knows in advance what man is going to do, what choice has man in the matter? Admittedly there are profound aspects to this question which are not altogether clear, but it is helpful to keep several things in mind:

First, man's will is always a relatively small part of any given circumstance. Man has no control over where he is born, into what family, or with what abilities or disabilities, advantages or disadvantages. He is subject to many influences beyond his control. He is rather like a baby in a playpen. He has real freedom, but only within certain prescribed bounds. Francis Schaeffer points out that when someone throws a man a ball, he can either catch it or let it fall. Barring some physical defect, he is not so limited that he has no power of decision or choice.

Second, God's foreknowledge (which is not to be confused with His election or with predestination) is not in itself the *cause* of what happens. For example, God foreknew that Demas would forsake the Apostle Paul for love of this world, but God's foreknowledge did not *predispose* Demas to turn back, much less *compel* him to do so. Demas acted in freedom; he made his own personal choice, under no compulsion.

Again, God foreknew that Saul would receive Christ and become Paul the Apostle, but on the Damascus Road, Saul exercised his own will in answering the Lord's summons. God foreknows your decisions before you make them—He knows what you will do and where you will go—but this foreknowledge does not interfere in the slightest with your complete freedom to act.

J.I. Packer calls this difficulty (reconciling divine sovereignty and human freedom) an *antinomy*, an apparent contradiction between conclusions that seem equally logical, reasonable, or necessary. He says:

> An antinomy exists when a pair of principles stand side by side, seemingly irreconcilable, yet both undeniable. There are cogent reasons for believing each of them: each rests on clear, solid evidence; but it is a mystery to you how they can be squared with each other. You see that each must be true on its own, but you do not see how they can both be true together. . . .
>
> Modern physics faces an antinomy, in this sense, in its study of light. There is cogent evidence to show that light consists of waves, and equally cogent evidence to show that it consists of particles. It is not apparent how light can be both waves and particles, but the evidence is there, and so neither view can be ruled out in favor of the other. Neither, however, can be reduced to the other or explained in terms of the other; the two seemingly incompatible positions must be held together, and both must be treated as true. Such a necessity scandalizes our tidy minds, no doubt, but there is no help for it if we are to be loyal to the facts.[12]

We may take comfort that divine sovereignty is exercised by a personal, all-loving, all-knowing God. But His sovereignty in no way lessens our freedom—or our privilege and responsibility to know and do His good will.

CHAPTER THREE

Jesus Christ

Dr. W.H. Griffith Thomas wrote a book entitled *Christianity Is Christ*. This title sums up the heart and uniqueness of Christianity.

Buddha is not essential to the teaching of Buddhism, or Muhammad to Islam, but everything about Christianity is determined by the person and work of Jesus Christ. Christianity owes its life and character in every detail to Christ. Its teachings are teachings about Him. He was the origin and will be the fulfillment of its hopes. He is the source of its ideas, which were born of what He said and did. The strength of Christ's church is the strength of His own Spirit, who is omnipotent.

But who is this Man, Jesus Christ? He Himself made His identity the central question of His ministry. He asked Peter, "Who do you say I am?" (Matt. 16:15) To be wrong at this point is fatal, as the history of the church has shown.

We must be clear, first, that Jesus Christ was fully God. He is expressly called God in various passages of Scripture, of which the following are a few examples: "The Word was God" (John 1:1; that the Word is Christ is confirmed in v. 14); "our great God and Saviour, Jesus Christ" (Titus 2:13); "His Son Jesus Christ. . . . the true God and eternal life" (1 John 5:20).

Christ Claimed Deity

Jesus claimed Deity for Himself in a way quite clear to His listeners. He said, on one occasion, "I and the Father are one" (John 10:30). His claim to deity was considered by the religious leaders to be blasphemy, and led to His crucifixion: "The Jews insisted, 'We have a law, and according to that law He must die, because He claimed to be the Son of God' " (John 19:7). The high priest expressly asked Christ, "Tell us if You are the Christ, the Son of God," and Jesus answered, "Yes, it is as you say" (Matt. 26:63-64). This was a clear affirmative answer, and the high priest said there was no further need of witnesses because they had heard His "blasphemy" with their own ears. He had said that "God [was] His own Father, making Himself equal with God" (John 5:18).

Jesus Christ claimed the prerogatives and authority of God. He said He had authority to forgive sins (Mark 2:10) and that He would come in the clouds of heaven, sitting at the right hand of power (Mark 14:62), implying authority to judge men: "The Father judges no one, but has entrusted all judgment to the Son" (John 5:22). Several times Jesus asserted that He Himself had the authority and power to raise the dead (John 6:39-40, 54; 10:17-18).

Jesus possessed attributes which belong to God alone. He claimed omnipotence, or all power (Matt. 28:18), and during His life He demonstrated this power over nature by stilling the stormy waves (Mark 4:39) and by turning water into wine (John 2:7-11); over physical disease (Mark 3:10); over the spirit world of demons (Luke 4:35); and over death by raising Lazarus from the grave (John 11:43-44). He also has power over all the heavenly hosts (Eph. 1:20-22).

He is omniscient, or all-knowing. He knew, as only God could know, what was in men's minds before they spoke (Mark 2:8; John 2:25). He is omnipresent, and promised to be with all His disciples to the end of the age (Matt. 28:20).

Christ the Creator

He is the Creator (John 1:3) and Sustainer (Heb. 1:3) of the universe. Perhaps the most comprehensive statement about the deity of Christ is that "In Christ all the fullness of the Diety lives in bodily form" (Col. 2:9).

Christ accepted the worship of men, which is due to God alone. He commended rather than rebuked doubting Thomas, who fell at His feet and declared in awe, "My Lord and my God!" (John 20:28) This was the same Jesus who scorned Satan's invitation to worship him by replying, "Worship the Lord your God, and serve Him only" (Matt. 4:10; cf. Deut. 6:13).

Another dimension of Christ's deity to be kept in mind is His preexistence. He did not *become* the Son of God either at His *birth* or sometime during His earthly life. He *was* and *is* the eternal Son, coexistent and coeternal with the Father. John declared, "In the beginning was the Word," and, "Through Him all things were made; without Him nothing was made that has been made" (John 1:1, 3). Jesus affirmed His preexistence when the Jews challenged Him about His age. "You're not fifty years old yet," they said; He replied, "I tell you the truth, before Abraham was born, I am!" (cf. John 8:57-58)

The deity of Christ is woven into the warp and woof of everything He said and taught. It is confirmed by what others clearly understood Him to say. The things that He did were conclusive evidence that His words were not clever deceit or the babblings of a demented person.

Christ Also Fully Man

But Jesus was not only fully God—He was also fully man, fully human. This is a vital aspect of the person of Christ. If He were not fully human, He could not have represented us on the cross, and He could not be the High Priest who comforts and strengthens us. But He *has* gone through our human experience (Heb. 2:16-18) and is fully able to understand us and sympathize with us.

Though His conception was supernatural, Jesus' birth was that of a normal child born of a human mother (Matt. 1:18). He is spoken of as being born of the seed of the woman (Gen. 3:15) and of the seed of Abraham (Heb. 2:16). In this way, in the Virgin Birth, "The Word became flesh" (John 1:14).

Jesus, as a normal child, grew physically and mentally. "And the child grew and became strong; He was filled with wisdom, and the grace of God was upon Him" (Luke 2:40).

Jesus referred to Himself as a man: "As it is, you are determined to kill Me, a Man who has told you the truth" (John 8:40). He was recognized by others as a man (Acts 2:22). He had a body, soul, and spirit, and shared our physical and emotional experiences.

Jesus got hungry (Matt. 4:2) and thirsty (John 19:28). His feet ached and He got weary from traveling (John 4:6). He needed sleep and refreshment (Matt. 8:24). He experienced and expressed love and compassion (Matt. 9:36). He was angry at those who defiled His Father's house (Matt. 21:13) and who deliberately refused the truth of God (Mark 3:5). He wept at the tomb of a dear friend (John 11:35), and as He faced the agony of the cross, He was troubled within (John 12:27).

The Son of Man

Jesus calls Himself the Son of Man eighty times in the Gospels. Though He claimed attributes of deity, He at the same time asserted His identification with *us* as sons of men. His humanity, in fact, was unique in that it was *complete*. Our Lord, as a man, according to A.H. Strong, was "free from both hereditary depravity and from actual sin, as is shown by His never offering sacrifice, never praying for [His own] forgiveness, teaching that all but He needed the new birth, challenging all to convict Him of a single sin."[1]

Christ's humanity was as real and genuine as His deity. Both must be maintained and neither may be emphasized at the expense of the other.

Mostly Man or Mostly God?

A brief review of church history will illustrate how easy it is to emphasize one aspect of Christ's nature over the other. Some of these tendencies are with us to this day, and we must guard against them. Heresies forced the early church to define clearly her belief in the deity and humanity of Christ. These definitions were not innovations, but merely crystallized what was already held to be biblical truth.

The Ebionites, early in the second century, denied the deity of Christ. They maintained He was merely a man, though perhaps supernaturally conceived. They conceded that, though a man, He held a peculiar relationship to God, especially from the time of His baptism when, they held, the fullness of the Holy Spirit rested on Him.

On the other hand, the docetists, later in the same century, denied Jesus' true humanity. They rejected the reality of His human body, suggesting it was merely a phantom that appeared to be human. This view was the logical conclusion of their assumption that matter is inherently evil. They implied that the divine Christ was not hungry and thirsty, nor did He suffer and die. Jesus' life on earth, they held, was largely an illusion.

The Arians, forerunners of today's Unitarians, mistook the biblical statements about Christ's subordination to the Father as teaching His inferiority. They taught that Christ was somehow created by the Father as the first and highest of created beings, but that He Himself was not eternally self-existent. This belief is current today in several major cults.

Another deviation was that of the Apollinarians, who were condemned at the Council of Constantinople in A.D. 381. Heavily influenced by Greek philosophy, Apollinarius taught that Christ had a true body and soul, and that in Him the place of the human mind or spirit was taken by His divine being. If this were true, however, it would mean that Jesus was not fully human and therefore was not tried or tempted in every respect as we are.

In the fifth century, Nestorius so emphasized the distinctness of Christ's two natures that he denied the real union between the divine and human in our Lord. He made this union a moral one rather than an organic one. Nestorians virtually believed in two natures and two persons instead of two natures in one person.

The Eutychians, on the other hand, were on the opposite

extreme, denying the distinction and coexistence of the two natures. They said that the divine and the human natures in Christ mingled into a third sort of nature, peculiar to Christ. They seemed to believe that Christ's human nature was really absorbed into His divine nature, though the divine nature was, by this "merger," somewhat changed from what it had been before the union. This group was condemned as heretical at the Council of Chalcedon in A.D. 451.

The question of the two natures of Christ is obviously complex, with numerous subtleties. The orthodox doctrine, promulgated at Chalcedon in 451, says that "in the one person, Jesus Christ, there are two natures, a human nature and a divine nature, each in its completeness and integrity, and that these two natures are organically and indissolubly united, yet so that no third nature is formed thereby. In brief, to use the antiquated dictum, orthodox doctrine forbids us either to divide the person or confound the natures."[2]

The deity and humanity of Christ's one Person is admittedly a profound subject, and it raises many questions. This concept is similar to that of the Trinity—we know by revelation that it is true, but have no satisfactory explanation.

In an attempt to explain Christ's two natures, some have suggested various "kenosis" theories. The term *kenosis* comes from the Greek word *kenoō* for *emptied* (Phil. 2:7). Some have contended that Christ totally emptied Himself of deity and was limited to the natural knowledge and ability of an ordinary man. Others have held that though He renounced His divine attributes, He still somehow possessed them. Still others have suggested that our Lord suspended His divine consciousness at His conception and reassumed it as a man. T.C. Hammond comments that "our Lord's attributes of deity were at no time laid aside. Any 'explanation' of His divine-human nature which violates the integrity of His deity is obviously to be rejected, and there seems to be no explanation that is without grave difficulties. The nearest we can get is that our Lord's perfect divine nature (with the possession of all its attributes) was so united with a perfect human nature that a single divine-human Personality developed with the divine element (if such a distinction can be made here) controlling the normal development of the human. Beyond this we cannot safely go."[3]

The early church creeds did not try to explain the mystery of how Christ's two natures were united in one Person. They recognized His full manhood and His true deity, but they did not solve the problem of bringing the two modes of His self-manifestation—manhood and deity—into the unity of a single person. From the beginning, it must have been obvious that the truth lay between two unacceptable tendencies—to break the Person into two, or to mingle the natures so that the result was neither truly human nor truly divine. In a statement which the early church found acceptable, and which has been used ever since, Athanasius said, "He became what He was not; He continued to be what He was." This is really a terse affirmation rather than an explanation.

In an effort to eliminate the difficulties that arise from the problem of Christ's two natures, some theologians, go to either of two extremes. Some exalt Christ's human nature to a level that would separate Him from the rest of humanity. For example, they say His nature was that of unfallen Adam. For this, there is no evidence in the Gospel records of His earthly life. Others, on the other hand, water down His deity. This view makes our Lord, on earth, subject to all human limitation—with, of course, the exception of sin.

"The factor that is forgotten, and may well be the only key to the problem, is the ministry of the Holy Spirit in the Person and life of Christ" according to Finlayson. "That Spirit, who had prepared His humanity and kept the unborn Child free from the taint of a mother's sin, never left Him, but throughout all the temptations and sufferings of His life and death brought to His human soul the light and comfort and strength which He needed to accomplish His task. In the light of that gracious ministry, we can understand, in some measure, how the divine nature was acting under human conditions, and how the human nature was acting in the fullest unity with the divine. That Spirit, who shared the eternal counsels of the Godhead, unified the consciousness of Christ so that there could be no possibility of division or dualism within Him. For this reason we can understand how there was nothing unnatural or unhuman about the self-consciousness of Jesus, even when He was in unbroken communion with the supernatural and eternal.

"However we explain it—and a full knowledge passes our comprehension—saving faith has always reached out to One who is perfect man, true God, and one Christ, and in the strength and fellowship of this faith we as Christians are called to abide."[4]

A proper knowledge of Christ's Person is crucial in understanding His work. If He were not the God-man, His work could not have eternal and personal significance for us.

What Christ Did

We have already considered the claims of our Lord to deity and the way He vindicated His claims by an authority over natural forces which could only have been supernatural. While fully appreciating who Jesus *is*, however, we must not overlook the equally important significance of what He has *done*—and is doing—for believers.

If Jesus were not fully God, He *could* not be our Saviour. But if He were God and yet did nothing on our behalf—that is, did not *do* something to bring us to God—He *would* not be our Saviour. Being God *qualified* Jesus Christ to be Saviour, but His atoning death for us *made* Him our Saviour. Jesus not only *could* save men; He *did*.

Christ was the perfect Man. As such, He was without sin in thought, word, or deed. He was able to challenge His enemies with the question, "Can any of you prove Me guilty of sin?" (cf. John 8:46) His foes had no reply. He was totally obedient to the Father. " 'My food,' said Jesus, 'is to do the will of Him who sent Me and to finish His work' " (John 4:34).

There are three reasons why our Lord's perfect life was a necessity.

1. It qualified Him to become the sacrificial offering for sin. Old Testament types all insist on the purity of the victim for sacrifice.

2. It meant that perfect obedience was rendered to God, in contrast to Adam's disobedience. Scripture emphasizes this repeatedly (Rom. 5:19; Heb. 10:6-7).

3. By it He became a qualified Mediator and High Priest for His people (Heb. 2:11-18).

Our Lord was, par excellence, "a Man with a mission." He frequently said, at a point of crisis, "My time has *not yet* come" (John 2:4, italics added; cf. 7:6). Finally He said, "The hour *has come* for the Son of Man to be glorified" (John 12:23, italics added). A little later, as He contemplated the awfulness of the cross, He said, "Now My heart is troubled, and what shall I say? Father, save Me from this hour'?" (John 12:27) The reason He had come, as He had said, was to "seek and to save what was lost" (Luke 19:10) and to "give His life as a ransom for many" (Mark 10:45). So central is the death of Christ to an understanding of Christianity that we will discuss it more fully in a later chapter.

Christ Left the Grave

But not only did our Lord live and die. The triumphant dynamic of Christianity is that He *arose from the dead.* The common greeting of the early church was the dramatic reminder, "He is risen!" The thing that changed a handful of cowardly, frightened disciples, who denied that they even knew their leader (Matt. 26:56, 70, 72, 74), into roaring lions proclaiming the faith, was the fact that they had seen Jesus, alive from the dead. Peter declared in Jerusalem, at the risk of his life, and just fifty days after the Resurrection, "God has raised this Jesus to life, and we are all witnesses of the fact" (Acts 2:32). Both the death and the resurrection of Christ show His supremacy and His uniqueness among all the religious leaders of the world.

A number of times Jesus predicted both His death and His resurrection (Mark 8:31; 10:32-34; cf. Matt. 16:21, etc.). But such a statement was so fantastic that the disciples didn't believe it until, after His entombment, they had the firsthand evidence of seeing Him themselves.

It is important to understand that the resurrection of Christ was a *bodily* resurrection, not one of "spirit" or "influence," as is sometimes suggested. The disciples, on first seeing Jesus after He rose, thought they were seeing a ghost and were terribly frightened. Our Lord had to say to them, "Look at My hands and My feet. It is I Myself! Touch Me and see; a ghost does not have flesh and bones, as you see I have" (Luke 24:39). He proceeded to eat fish and honey with them to further demonstrate His physical reality. He invited doubting Thomas to put his finger in the nailprints and put his hand in the pierced side (John 20:27), so giving further testimony to the physical nature of His resurrection body and also indicating that this was the body that had been crucified and buried.

His risen body, however, differed from our bodies and from His own previous body. For instance, our risen Lord passed through closed doors when He met with the disciples for the first time in the Upper Room (John 20:19). Paul discusses at some length the subject of the Resurrection and the resurrection body (1 Cor. 15). This passage should be studied carefully.

Resurrection Implications

The implications of the Resurrection are enormous. We should understand them as fully as possible—and *enjoy* them.

First, as we have seen, the Resurrection fully confirms the truth and value of what Jesus taught and did. Paul says, "And if Christ has not been raised, your faith is futile; you are still in your sins" (1 Cor. 15:17). Because of the Resurrection, we know we are not trusting in a myth; we know that our sins are actually forgiven through the death of Christ. Certainty and forgiveness are based on the empty tomb! Christ is the only One who has ever come back from death to tell men about the beyond. In *His* words we know we have the authoritative Word of God Himself.

Second, Christ's resurrection is the guarantee of our own resurrection. Jesus said, "Because I live, you also will live" (John 14:19). We know with assurance that the grave is not our end, and that we shall be raised as He was.

Third, we know that the body is in itself good, not inherently evil, as some have mistakenly thought. The fact that our Lord became flesh and took a physical body in the Incarnation shows this. It is confirmed by the Resurrection, which tells us that in the eternal state, body and soul will be reunited, though the body will, of course, be a glorified body like our Lord's. Christ is the One "who . . . will transform our lowly bodies so that they will be like His glorious body" (Phil. 3:21).

Fourth, we have assurance of the contemporary power of Christ in life today. We do not believe in a dead Christ hanging on a cross or lying in a grave, but in the risen Christ of the empty tomb. Christ gives us His life in salvation. This is the contemporary power, the dynamic, of Christian faith.

Many attempts have been made to explain away the Resurrection. A full discussion cannot be gone into here.

In summary, we can say that some false theories of the Resurrection (such as the swoon theory) revolve around denial of Christ's actual death. Other views hold that the disciples made an honest error which led them sincerely but wrongly to proclaim that Jesus had risen from the dead.

But all attempts to explain away the Resurrection flounder on the rocks of the actual evidence. Christ would have been a deceiver had He only swooned and allowed the disciples to think He had actually risen from the dead. The disciples were not prepared for a hallucination. They didn't *expect* He *would* rise and they didn't *believe* He *had* risen from the dead. They had to be persuaded against their "better judgment" that it was so (Luke 24:36-45). Furthermore, Christ appeared ten different times, in different places, and in one case to more than 500 people at once. Such an event cannot be explained by "hallucination." Also, the disciples would have been deceivers if they had stolen Christ's body. Nearly all of them died for their faith, however, in martyrdom. People will die for what they mistakenly *think* is true, but they don't die for what they *know* is false. The inability of the enemies of Christ to produce His body is further evidence that it had not been stolen.

The empty tomb, the revolutionized lives of the disciples, the Lord's Day (worship being shifted from Saturday to Sunday because of the Resurrection), the existence of the Christian church (which can be traced back to approximately A.D. 30)—all are conclusive evidence that the Resurrection is fact, not fiction. The final evidence is the transformation of those today who have met and been given new life by the risen Christ.

Ascension, Exaltation

Jesus not only predicted His death and resurrection, but also His ascension and exaltation (John 6:62; 17:1). In the Ascension, He visibly left His disciples and the earth and returned to heaven, forty days after His resurrection. His exit from this life was as miraculous as His entrance. The account of it is given in Acts 1:9-11.

Christ having ascended, God the Father gave Him a place of exaltation in heaven. God has "seated Him at His right hand in the heavenly realms, far above all rule and authority, power and dominion, and every title that can be given" (Eph. 1:20-21). Christ has a position of power and glory. His ascension and exaltation were necessary for the completion of His work of redemption. As the ascended and exalted Christ, He has entered heaven as a forerunner for us (Heb. 6:20). We are to follow Him. He is able to enter into the heavenly counterpart of the holy of holies in the earthly tabernacle because of the merits of His atonement. Believers will be able to follow Him because the blood of His atonement has been applied to them.

Christ is now before God as our High Priest and Advocate, "to appear for us in God's presence" (Heb. 9:24). "If anyone does sin, we have One who speaks to the Father in our defense—Jesus Christ, the Righteous One" (1 John 2:1). As our Mediator or Advocate (KJV), Christ is now active for us before the throne of God.

Christ has gone to prepare a place for us in heaven. He clearly told the disciples, "I will come back and take you to be with Me that you also may be where I am" (John 14:3). Every Christian should look forward with deep anticipation to the return of his Lord for him.

Because of the ascension and exaltation of Christ, we have

free and confident access into the very presence of God. We can "approach the throne of grace with confidence" (Heb. 4:16). In Old Testament times, access to the presence of God was limited to one person—the high priest; to one place—the holy of holies in the tabernacle (or the temple); and to one time—the Day of Atonement. But because Christ is our High Priest and has passed into the heavens, *each* of us has access to the Creator at *any* time and at *any* place. How the angels must wonder that we make so little use of this privilege of audience with the King!

Christianity is Christ from beginning to end. To know who Christ is and what He has done is to increase our awe, wonder, and appreciation of the One who, though He was rich, for our sakes became poor, that we through His poverty might become rich (2 Cor. 8:9).

CHAPTER FOUR

Christ's Death

hristianity is Christ, and unless we understand the death of Christ, we cannot possibly appreciate why our Lord came into human history. Without the death of Christ, there could be no forgiveness of sins and hence no salvation. Jesus Himself said, "For the Son of Man came to seek and to save what was lost" (Luke 19:10) and, "The Son of Man did not come to be served, but to serve, and to give His life as a ransom for many (Mark 10:45), clearly pointing to the redemptive nature of His death.

In the death of Christ, we have another "uniqueness" of Christianity. Here God has done for man what man cannot do for himself. God provided a way by which man, who is sinful and corrupt, can be forgiven, cleansed, and brought into vital and intimate relationship with his Maker—not on the basis of something *man* must do, but on the basis of what God Himself, in His Son, has *done.*

Every other religious system in the world is essentially a "do-it-yourself " proposition. Only in Christianity is salvation a free gift, offered not because man deserves it but because of the incomprehensible goodness of God's love. The Cross of Christ is the central fact of human history. His death is the basis for His personal worthiness to receive the worship of the whole creation (Rev. 5:9, 12-13).

Christ's death is a central theme of the Scriptures, both Old Testament and New. As far back as the Garden of Eden, when God cursed the serpent, He promised the Deliverer (Gen. 3:15). The Prophet Isaiah gives us a clear promise of One who would die for our sins: "But He was pierced for our transgressions . . . [and] crushed for our iniquities; the punishment that brought us peace was upon Him, and by His wounds we are healed. We all, like sheep, have gone astray, each of us has turned to his own way; and the Lord has laid on Him the iniquity of us all" (Isa. 53:5-6).

After His resurrection, Jesus joined two of His disciples walking toward Emmaus. Not recognizing Him, they revealed how puzzled they were by the recent events of Jesus' trial and death. Jesus chided them for not knowing Old Testament writings pointing to His death (Luke 24:25-27). These prophets, according to 1 Peter 1:10-12, were writing without knowing exactly who Christ was or when He would come. They were writing for others who would read their message later—people such as the two disciples and those of us today.

Some question the necessity to *understand* the meaning of the Atonement. After all, they argue, we are not saved by any theory of the Atonement, but by the actual death of Christ. This, of course, is true. We must be careful not to try to reduce the Atonement into merely a neat formula. On the other hand, just as what we believe about Christ's person is crucial—even though we are saved by what He has *done*—so it is important for us to understand the meaning of His mission to die for man's sin. Otherwise we may find ourselves wittingly or unwittingly opposing the Gospel in one of its most vital and fundamental teachings.

Old Testament Background

A clear understanding of the significance of the death of Christ requires an understanding of the Old Testament background which led up to it.

Man is hopelessly separated from God because of his sin: "But your iniquities have separated you from your God; your

sins have hidden His face from you, so that He will not hear"
(Isa. 59:2). God takes the initiative and provides the way by
which our estrangement may be ended. Leon Morris comments, "In the Old Testament, [atonement] is usually said to
be obtained by the sacrifices, but it must never be forgotten
that God says of the atoning blood, 'I have given it to you
upon the altar to make an atonement for your souls' (Lev.
17:11, KJV, italics added). Atonement is secured not by any
value inherent in the sacrificial victim but because sacrifice is
the divinely appointed way of securing atonement."[1]

The whole sacrificial system of the Old Testament was a
symbolic portrayal of what would be completely fulfilled in
Christ. The Passover, celebrated at the time of the Exodus of
the Israelites from Egypt, is the fullest picture. Each believing
family slew a perfect lamb and put its blood on the doorposts
and lintels of the house. The angel of death, when he saw the
blood, passed over that household, which in this way escaped
the judgment of having its firstborn die. As with other sacrifices, the elements of perfection, the shedding of blood, and
substitution were all present.

Christ was the fulfillment of all that the Passover lamb stood
for. He was "the Lamb of God, who takes away the sin of the
world" (John 1:29). Those who in faith offered animal sacrifices in Old Testament times looked forward to the coming
Messiah, just as we by faith look back to the Cross of Christ.
The animal sacrifices did not save, but faith in what they
symbolized *did*. We by faith lay hold on the fulfillment of the
symbols. As Isaac Watts wrote:

> Not all the blood of beasts
>   On Jewish altars slain
> Could give the guilty conscience peace,
>   Or wash away the stain.
> But Christ the heavenly Lamb
>   Takes all our sins away;
> A sacrifice of nobler name
>   And richer blood than they.

Atonement for Sin

Christ's death is spoken of as the atonement for our sin. It has been suggested that *atonement* means, basically, "at-one-ment" —that is to say, a bringing together of those who are estranged. But the Old Testament word means, essentially, "to cover." The animal sacrifices provided a "covering" for sin until the death of Christ would put it forever away.

In the New Testament, various ideas are presented which explain and illustrate the Atonement. It is spoken of as a *reconciliation:* "When we were God's enemies, we were reconciled to Him [God] through the death of His Son" (Rom. 5:10; cf. 2 Cor. 5:18-19; Eph. 2:16; Col. 1:20). Reconciliation implies former hostility between the reconciled parties. As sinners, we were enemies of God. God, because of His holy character, is opposed to that which is sinful and unholy. The death of Christ did away with the cause of God's enmity by taking away our sin. We have been reconciled to God, the root cause of alienation having been removed and our attitude toward God having been changed. God has always loved us, and still loves us. But His wrath—the fixed, permanent attitude of God's holiness against evil—has been turned away from us. It has been carried by Christ.

The death of Christ is also spoken of as a *propitiation:* "God presented Him as a sacrifice of atonement, through faith in His blood. He did this to demonstrate His justice, because in His forebearance He had left the sins committed beforehand unpunished" (Rom. 3:25). Propitiation has within it the concept of "the removing of wrath by the offering of a gift,"[2] as Morris wrote. It has a personal quality to it. A young man might propitiate his girlfriend, for example, by sending her a bouquet of roses. God, in this case, is propitiated because the perfect sacrifice of Christ, in laying down His life for us, has fully met the holy and just requirements of God's Law.

It is important to understand that God does not first reconcile us and then love us. Rather, *because* God has loved us, He reconciles us and opens the way for propitiation.

Ransom is another term used to define the death of Christ. It is closely linked with the idea of redemption. "[Christ] gave

Christ's Death

Himself a ransom for all man—the testimony given in its proper time" (1 Tim. 2:6; cf. 1 Peter 1:18). Though some church leaders seem to have thought this ransom was paid to Satan, the general conviction has been that it is the price paid to meet the holy requirements of God's Law and redeem us from its curse. "You know that it was not with perishable things such as silver or gold . . . but with the precious blood of Christ, a lamb without blemish or defect" (1 Peter 1:18-19).

Our Substitute

Among the various terms that give the clearest explanations of the death of Christ is *substitute*. "Christ died for sins once for all, the righteous for the unrighteous, to bring you to God" (1 Peter 3:18). Christ died *for* us—that is, in our place. "God made Him who had no sin to be sin for us, so that in Him we might become the righteousness of God" (2 Cor. 5:21). The whole concept of sacrifice for sin carries with it the idea of substitution, which is fulfilled in Christ, "who bore our sins in His body on the tree, so that we might die to sins and live for righteousness; by His wounds you have been healed" (1 Peter 2:24).

In the doctrinal statements of many Bible-believing churches and institutions, specific and particular mention is made of the "substitutionary" atonement of Christ. The reason for this is that other interpretations of the Atonement have been advanced which, though some of them contain partial truth, have tended to eclipse, if not deny outright, the central truth of substitutionary atonement. Some theologians openly attack this doctrine, suggesting that the idea of substitution is a Pauline addition to the teaching of Christ. Even from the small portion of Scripture we have examined, however, it is clear that such claims are not the case. The teaching that Christ has taken our place and suffered and died in our behalf is as present in the Gospels as in the rest of the New Testament.

Often the viewpoint of a speaker, minister, or author on the substitutionary atonement is a reliable indicator of the orthodoxy of his other theological views.

Among the many perverted views of the Atonement are the following:

1. The *moral influence* or *example* theory. The idea here is that man needs only to repent and reform to be reconciled to God. Advocates of this view believe the death of Christ is merely the powerful example of a man committed to truth and righteousness at all costs, and that we are redeemed as we allow His example to have a determining influence on our own efforts at moral improvement.

There is, of course, great moral influence in Christ's example. It is true that "Christ suffered for you, leaving you an example, that you should follow in His steps" (1 Peter 2:21). But Scripture clearly teaches not only that sin has defiled us personally, but that because of it we are guilty before a holy God. Many passages of Scripture clearly teach that Christ died *for our sins,* and the moral influence theory ignores these passages entirely.

Other Erroneous Views

2. The *governmental* theory holds that the Atonement is a requirement of God's government of the universe, which "cannot be maintained, nor can the divine law preserve its authority over its subjects, unless the pardon of the offenders is accompanied by some exhibition of the high estimate which God sets upon His law and on the heinous guilt of violating it."¹ But why is *Christ* necessary, if this is all there is to the Atonement? And why should One who is *perfect* suffer, rather than one who is *guilty?*

It is true that the Cross shows man, with extreme vividness, the awfulness of sin, and that it is eloquent testimony that man may not ignore or toy with the Law of God. But this surely is incidental to Christ's being made sin for us so that we may be made the righteousness of God in Him (2 Cor. 5:21). This view also fails to do justice to all the passages of Scripture already referred to.

3. Some have felt that the crucifixion of Christ was simply an untimely *accident of history,* unexpected and unforeseen. But

Scripture clearly contradicts this view. Christ Himself assured His disciples that it was for this purpose that He had come into the world (John 12:27). In the Garden of Gethsemane, He prayed to His Heavenly Father, "Yet not as I will, but as You will" (Matt. 26:39). He says further, "The reason My Father loves Me is that I lay down My life—only to take it up again. No one takes it from Me, but I lay it down of My own accord. I have authority to lay it down and authority to take it up again" (John 10:17-18). The prophets predicted the Messiah's sacrificial death and, in fact, all scriptural evidence opposes the idea that Christ's death was accidental. That Christ did not *have* to die, but *voluntarily* endured the cross for us, is one of the central and most moving aspects of His sacrifice.

4. Others would suggest that though Christ's death might have been anticipated by sensitivity to the gathering storm, He died, essentially, as *another martyr* of history. But if this were the case, how could forgiveness come from His death, and how do we account for Jesus' statement, when He began the ceremony we celebrate as the Lord's Supper, "This is My blood of the covenant, which is poured out for many for the forgiveness of sins"? (Matt. 26:28) The whole emphasis of the Scripture is opposed to any view of the Cross that is less than supernatural.

The idea of substitution is a basic theme throughout the Bible. There are other lessons to be learned from the Atonement, to be sure, but none is so prominent as to obscure this basic and wonderful truth.

Objections to Substitution

There have always been objections to the substitutionary atonement, and we should consider some of them.

Some insist that if God does not pardon sin without requiring atonement, He must either not be all-powerful or else not be a God of love. "Why can't He simply forgive sin out of His pure mercy?" skeptics want to know. "Could not an all-powerful God, in His omnipotence, have redeemed the world as easily as He created it? Since God commands man to forgive freely, why does He Himself not freely forgive?"

Finlayson summarizes the answer given such questions by Anselm in the twelfth century: "God cannot so forgive because He is not a private person, but God. God's will is not His own in the sense that anything is permissible to Him or becomes right because He wills it. What God determines is what God does. God cannot deal with sin except as in His holiness He sees it to be. If He did not punish it, or make adequate satisfaction for it, then He would be forgiving it unjustly."[4]

It is important to realize, as we have previously pointed out, that God exercises all His attributes in harmony with each other. His holiness demands atonement for sin. His love provides it. God's attributes never violate one another, nor are they antagonistic to each other. They are not in an uneasy equilibrium, but they work together in full and complete harmony. "Mercy is shown not by trampling upon the claims of justice, but by vicariously satisfying them."[5] In the Cross of Christ, "Love and faithfulness meet together; righteousness and peace kiss each other" (Ps. 85:10).

Love and Holiness

The New Testament speaks of the "wedding," or coming together, of the attributes of God's love and holiness in the Cross of Christ so that He could be "just and the One who justifies those who have faith in Jesus" (Rom. 3:26). In the very act of forgiving sin, or, to use Paul's "daring word . . . of 'justifying the ungodly,' God must act in harmony with His whole character. He must show what He is in relation to sin— that evil cannot dwell with Him because He refuses to tolerate sin in any form. In the very process of making forgiveness available to men, He must show His complete abhorrence of sin. In other words, God must not merely forgive men, but must forgive in a way which shows that He forever hates evil and can never treat it as other than completely hateful. Sin makes a real difference to God, and even in forgiving, He cannot ignore sin or regard it as other or less than it is. If He did so, He would not be more gracious than He is in the Atonement—He would cease to be God."[6]

Others have said that the very idea of God's permitting *Christ* to die for *our* sin, as an innocent victim for guilty sinners, was injustice rather than justice. Some go so far as actually to call it immoral. But such charges would be true only if Christ were an unwilling victim. As we have seen, the glory of the Cross is in the *voluntary* nature of Christ's coming to earth. "He did not consider equality with God a thing to be grasped, but humbled Himself and became obedient to death, even the death of the cross" (cf. Phil. 2:6-8). Hammond observes, "The Sufferer must have a double connection between God and Himself on the one hand, and the sinner and Himself on the other."[7] Only a solidly scriptural objection could fairly be raised against evangelical teaching on this subject.

Though we must consider alternative interpretations, we must note that critics approach the doctrine of substitution from their preconceived notions of what God *ought to have done* and their own superficial and humanistic ethical standards.

Other Questions

In addition to the objections we have already mentioned, certain other questions may come to your mind about the substitutionary death of Christ. How, for example, could the death of one Person possibly atone for the innumerable sins of the whole world?

At the human level, such atonement would obviously be impossible. One person may die for one other, but for no more than one other. But when we consider the effectiveness of the death of Christ, we must remember who died. Christ was not merely a man; He was the God-man: "God was in Christ" (2 Cor. 5:19). Christ's life was of infinite value, and His death likewise had infinite worth. The sum total of the value of all of those for whom He died does not approximate the infinite value of the divine life that was given at Calvary in sacrifice for their sakes.

In the "value" of the One who died is also the answer to the question, "Since Christ was only dead for three days, how can His experience be compared with the eternal death millions will experience if they do not trust Him?" The death Christ died was an infinite death, both in value and in the intensity of the spiritual suffering the Son of God went through. We simply cannot comprehend what it must have been for the sinless Son of God to become sin (2 Cor. 5:21) for us.

There is also the question as to whether, when Christ died, it is true to say that "God died." Robert J. Little points out, in answer to this question, that Christ "became a man in order to die, for without dying as a man, He could not have delivered men from the penalty of sin. . . . Yet when He died, His *divine being* did not die. And when He died as a man, it was only His body which died. Scripture makes it clear that when *any* human being dies, it is the body which dies. The soul and spirit live on. Hence, when Christ died, we do not say that God died, though He who died on the cross was God. No finite mind can fully understand everything about the infinite God, but we can have some understanding of what is involved."[8]

A number of clear implications arise out of an understanding of the Atonement.

One is that in the Atonement we are dealing with an absolute issue of life and death. The Bible clearly tells us that "the wages of sin is death, but the gift of God is eternal life in Christ Jesus our Lord" (Rom. 6:23). Some tend to hedge on drawing lines between those who are saved and those who are lost. This hedging is perhaps due to their reluctance to judge individuals and perhaps also because of their incipient hope that all are saved.

It is true that only the Lord knows those who are His, and that our judgment, based on a man's profession in words and on the external nature of his life, may be faulty. But the Scripture knows no such vagueness. "Whoever believes in the Son *has eternal life*, but whoever rejects the Son *will not see life*, for God's wrath remains on him" (John 3:36, italics added). Men are in sin and Christ died for their sin. A man is *now* either in Christ by faith, or still in sin because of unbelief. There is no in-between ground. A person has either life or death, lives either in light or in darkness, is either saved or lost.

Other Implications

It is in the death of Christ that we can see clearly why some widespread ideas of the universal fatherhood of God are errone-ous. Often accompanying a reluctance to draw distinctions, people who hold these ideas suggest that all men are God's children and that therefore efforts to "convert" them are in bad taste. But though we all *are* God's offspring by creation (Acts 17:28), we are not God's children spiritually, else the Atone-ment would have been unnecessary. Jesus spoke sharply to those who refused to recognize Him as God, saying, "You be-long to your father, the devil" (John 8:44). On the other hand, "to all who received Him, to those who believed in His name, He gave the right *to become* the children of God" (John 1:12, italics added). We cannot *become* what we already *are*.

The death of Christ is what makes the Gospel good *news* rather than good *advice*. Christ did not die for us because we recognized our need and cried out to God for help. "But God demonstrates His own love for us in this: While we were still sinners, Christ died for us" (Rom. 5:8). The Gospel is not a set of swimming instructions for a drowning man, but a pardon and reprieve from death for a man who is undeserving. There is nothing we must or can *do* to benefit from it, except simply to receive it as a free gift and so experience eternal life.

The Atonement is what gives a Christian his basis for assur-ance of forgiveness of sin and eternity in heaven. This assur-ance is not arrogant presumption that we are better than any-one else, but rather confidence, based on God's own Word, in what Christ has done for us by dying on the cross. From the cross, just before He died, Jesus said, "It is finished" (John 19:30). So we speak of the *"finished* work of Christ," believing that our Lord has already done everything necessary for our salvation. We still need daily cleansing and forgiveness of sin, of course, and we receive it when we confess our sin (1 John 1:9). But we receive forgiveness on the basis of what has al-ready been accomplished in us—as sons, not as alienated sin-ners. God intends us to be assured of our salvation: "I write these things to you who believe in the name of the Son of God so *that you may know* that you have eternal life" (1 John 5:13, italics added).

Assurance need not lead to indifference and smug content-
ment. It can also result in deep joy and a loving response to
Christ. We are continually reminded, "You are not your own;
you were bought at a price. Therefore honor God with your
body" (1 Cor. 6:19-20). The new life we receive changes our
attitudes, motives, values, and will. In ourselves we are incapable of such changes, but in Christ we become new creations
(2 Cor. 5:17). It is for this reason that Paul was so adamant in
maintaining that the church add nothing to simple trust as a
requirement for salvation, and add nothing afterward by way of
legal regulation to maintain salvation. The Gospel is not
Christ "plus" something, as good as something may be, but
Christ *alone* in His atoning death for us.

Demonstrates God's Love

The Atonement also demonstrates the nature and character of
God's love. We live in a world which is acutely aware of man's
pain, suffering, and misery. No one is interested in a God who
is aloof and untouched by human need, or even in a God who
might save sinners from a distance. In the Cross of Christ the
affirmation, "God is love," takes concrete expression. People
will believe a demonstration of love in action before they will
believe a person who declares it only in words. John says,
"This is how we know what love is: Jesus Christ laid down His
life for us" (1 John 3:16).

God, in Christ, became involved in this life. He assumed its
burdens and entered into its tragedies. Finally Christ took on
full responsibility for this life by "becoming sin for us so that in
Him we might become the righteousness of God" (2 Cor.
5:21). Through the Atonement, we *know* that God is not
indifferent to man's tragedy and suffering.

Christ's death, in its objective accomplishment and subjective impact, is the central fact of history.

> Love so amazing, so divine
> Demands my soul, my life, my all.
> CHARLES WESLEY

CHAPTER FIVE

Man and Sin

hat is man?" asked the Psalmist David, centuries ago. It is striking that this is also the burning question of the twentieth century and the Space Age. Is man merely a glorified animal? Is he merely the sum total of all his chemicals and their reactions? Or is he more than this?

As the genetic code is deciphered and the electronic aspects of the brain's functioning are understood, the problem becomes increasingly urgent.

"Who am I?" The piercing question of identity must be answered by every person. Our answer, whether we realize it or not, has enormous influence upon our thinking and acting, our outlook, and our living. Never was it more important for a Christian to understand what the Bible says about man in order to have an anchor on the sea of human speculation.

The first question to be answered is that of man's origin. Where did he come from? "In the beginning God created the heavens and the earth" (Gen. 1:1), says the Bible, and, "God said, 'Let Us make man in Our image, in Our likeness; and let them rule over the fish of the sea, and the birds of the air, over the livestock, over all the earth, and over all the creatures that move along the ground.' So God created man in His own image, in the image of God He created him; male and female

61

He created them" (vv. 26-27).

Scripture consistently teaches that neither the universe nor man himself is the product of blind chance. Man especially is the result of careful and purposeful deliberation on the part of the members of the Triune Godhead.

Adam, the first man, was created in God's image. *Adam* is a proper name, but the Hebrew term from which it comes also has the connotation of "mankind." It is frequently so used in the Old Testament.

God said, "It is not good for the man to be alone," and to complement man, He made a woman to be Adam's helper (Gen. 2:18, 22).

"By faith we understand that the universe was formed at God's command, so that what is seen was not made out of what was visible" (Heb. 11:3). In other words, God created matter *ex nihilo* (out of nothing). He then formed matter into living objects—plants, animals, and man.

The Bible does not claim to tell us *how* man and the universe were created. It does, however, assert emphatically and unambiguously *that God brought them into being.* Nowhere does the Bible attempt to *prove* God. It *assumes* Him. A Christian unashamedly begins with the assumption that God exists. He is convinced that the life, death, and resurrection of Christ clearly bear out this assumption. Such assumption is not naive or unintellectual, and we should keep in mind that unbelievers who reject the biblical view of Creation also begin with presuppositions and assumptions on which they base *their* claims. *Everyone* begins somewhere with an assumption that is not provable in the scientific sense.

It is also important to realize that New Testament writers saw Adam as a person as historical as our Lord Himself. Paul clearly considered Adam to be a distinct individual as well as the prototype of fallen man (Rom. 5:12-21; 1 Cor. 15:22). Our Lord spoke about the creation of man, confirming the Genesis account (Matt. 19:4). There is no room for mythical or allegorical interpretations of the historicity of Adam's creation and subsequent fall.

Man was distinct and unique from the rest of creation. He

was to subdue it and have dominion over it. He is at the top of all living beings. Man's self-consciousness, his capacity for intelligent reasoning, and, above all, his moral and spiritual sense, set him completely apart from all other creatures. No creature other than man has ever been observed building a chapel.

Body, Soul, and Spirit

Genesis 2 gives further information on the creation of man: "The Lord God formed the man from the dust of the ground and breathed into his nostrils the breath of life, and the man became a living being" (v. 7). It is clear that two elements were involved in man's creation. One is "the dust of the ground." The other is "the breath of life," which was given by God. The union of these two elements makes man a living being.

Man is clearly more than one substance. But are the components of his being *three* (body, soul, and spirit) or *two* (body and soul)? The Old Testament does not have a fixed term for the immaterial part of man's nature. The terms *soul, heart,* and *spirit* are used as counterparts of the material side. Along with the term *body,* they include the whole man. David wrote, "My *soul* thirsts for You, my *body* longs for You" (Psalm 63:1, italics added). But not all such biblical expressions indicate a twofold nature of man. Others just as plainly speak of *three* aspects of man's being: "My *soul* yearns, even faints for the courts of the Lord; my *heart* and my *flesh* cry out for the living God" (Ps. 84:2, italics added).

Should the God-breathed part of man be viewed as *two* parts—i.e., *soul* and *spirit* separately—or as *one?* Hammond observes: " 'Soul' and 'spirit' are certainly not to be regarded as synonymous in scriptural language. But, on the other hand, they are not kept invariably distinct. Compare Psalm 74:19 with Ecclesiastes 3:21; Matthew 10:28 with Luke 23:46; Acts 2:27 with 7:59. The references [used for a threefold] division are . . . 1 Thessalonians 5:23; Hebrews 4:12; cf. Luke 1:46-47. . . . But those who suggest [such a division] admit that soul and spirit, in the body, are separable only in thought. It would seem best to regard them as differing aspects of the same essence, and to remember that whatever distinctions are made for the spiritual purposes of scriptural teaching, there is a substratum which is common to both soul and spirit."[1]

Man a Unity

In any case, the Bible always views man as a unity, both material and immaterial. The Resurrection shows that man is as essentially body as he is essentially soul or spirit. The notion that man is a soul imprisoned in a body is a Greek concept, not a biblical one.

What does it mean that man was created in the image and likeness of God? It certainly does not mean that he has any *physical* likeness to God. Scripture clearly teaches that God is a Spirit and does not have physical parts like a man (John 4:24). The Bible uses anthropomorphic expressions, such as "the hand of God," only to accommodate our human incapacity to think in any other terms. The strong prohibition against man's representing God by graven images was given because no one had ever seen God and therefore could not know how He looks. Nothing on earth *could* represent Him (Deut. 4:15-23).

The image of God in man has to do, rather, with *personality.* Man has "a free, self-conscious, rational, and moral personality like that of God—a nature capable of distinguishing right and wrong, of choosing the right and rejecting the wrong, and of ascending to the heights of spiritual attainment and communion with God," according to D.M. Edwards.[2]

The original man was intelligent. He could give names to all the animals when they were presented to him (Gen. 2:19-20). He had the power of reasoning and thought. In speaking, he could connect words and ideas. He had moral and spiritual qualities. He could and did commune with God and had the power to resist moral evil or yield to it (Gen. 3).

Because man has been created in the image of God, human life is inviolate. God instituted capital punishment (Gen. 9:6) for this reason.

The new man is *renewed* in the image of God in righteousness (Eph. 4:23-24; Col. 3:10). The implication of "renewed"
is that man once had a moral likeness to God, but that it was
lost. Originally man was holy and the basic inclination of his
nature was toward God. He was not *neutral* toward God, for
the creation of the "new man" is after the pattern of the
original. Nevertheless, from the beginning man had freedom to
choose evil, and so to sin.

At the same time it is important to realize that man was also
free *not* to sin. He had no original inward tendency to sin, as
we have. Though he was capable of being tempted, he was
neither *compelled* nor *impelled* to sin. Adam *chose* to do so
deliberately, as a free act. In the words of the famous phrase,
man did not have inability to sin; he had ability *not* to sin.

Image vs. Likeness

Roman Catholics and some others distinguish between "image"
and "likeness" because both words are used in Genesis 1:26.
They have suggested that the *image* of God in man is only in
his personality, and that the *likeness* of God is a supernatural
gift given man by God in creation—i.e., "an original righteousness and perfect self-determination before God which
could be, and indeed was, lost in the Fall. The *image*, on the
other hand, consists of what belongs to man by nature, i.e., his
free will, rational nature, and dominion over the animal world,
which could not be lost even in the Fall. This would mean that
the Fall destroyed what was originally supernatural in man, but
left his nature and the image of God in him wounded, and his
will free."[3]

This distinction, however, is not borne out by Scripture.
The word *image* is used alone in Genesis 1:27 to describe what
is meant by the two terms together in verse 26. In a similar
construction elsewhere (Gen. 5:1), the word *likeness* is used
alone.

Had things remained as they were in the original Creation,
all would have been well. Sin and death, with all their disastrous consequences for the human race, would never have

come into being if Adam and Eve had chosen to obey rather than disobey by asserting their wills against God. But they *did* assert themselves against God, and their rebellion brought titanic disaster to all their descendants.

It is significant and intensely interesting that most, if not all, primitive religious traditions have, in one form or another, a belief in such a cataclysmic event. The Fall permanently altered what previously was an idyllic relationship between God and man. Man is generally viewed as having intimate fellowship with his Creator. But ever since he offended Him, he has suffered from God's displeasure as well as from the loss of fellowship that resulted from his estrangement. Even in primitive animistic societies, which worship many gods, there is belief in a high-sky God who is the Creator. Since the passing of the golden age of intimate contact, this God is aloof from man. He now deals with human beings only through the lesser gods. All of these ideas seem to be echoes and reflections—distorted, faint, or mutilated by the passage of time—of the event, clearly described in the Bible (Gen. 3), which we call the Fall.

Personal Responsibility

The sin of Adam and Eve, as we have seen, was something for which they were personally responsible. They did not have sinful natures such as we have, so the temptation to sin must have come from outside them. The Bible describes this source as "the serpent" (Gen. 3:1), a term scripturally identified with Satan (Rev. 12:9). The Fall really explains how sin entered the human race, rather than how evil got into the world.

The ultimate answer to the profound question of the origin of evil is wrapped in the mysteries of God's counsels. Why did God not prevent evil from entering the universe, since He knew in advance what would happen? Why did He not make man incapable of sinning? He *could* have, but had He done so, we would not be human beings with freedom of choice. We would be robots, or "talking dolls" that always speak the same word when someone pulls the string.

Though we have no final answers to sin's origin, God knew what would happen and, as someone has said, "thought it was worth the risk." C.S. Lewis observed that it is useless to speculate endlessly about the *origin* of evil. Each of us, however, faces the *fact* of evil, and the whole of God's redemptive program has to do with combating it. God is not the author of sin. Had our first parents not disobeyed Him, sin would never have entered the human race.

The several facets of sin are clear in the progression which is described in Genesis 3. Adam and Eve are first tempted to *doubt* God's Word ("Did God really say?"), then led on to *disbelieve* it ("You will not surely die"), and finally to *disobey* it by eating fruit from the forbidden tree.

The results of man's disobedience were immediate and obvious—separation from God and awareness of guilt. The curse which God pronounced involved, for mankind, both physical and spiritual death, hard physical labor, and sorrow. Man's fall involved the whole natural creation as well (cf. Rom. 8:21-22).

As a result of the Fall, the image of God in man was badly marred in both its moral and its natural dimensions. Man lost his original inclination toward God and became a perverted creature, inclined away from his Creator. His intellect became bound, his emotions corrupted, and his will enslaved. Men speak about man as "evolving" from a primitive condition, but the Bible (Rom. 1:18-32) graphically portrays his *descent* rather than *ascent*.

"Total Depravity"

The result was "total depravity." This expression of man's condition after the Fall has been widely misunderstood, with the result that the Christian position regarding man's sinful nature has sometimes been unjustly caricatured. The doctrine of depravity "was never intended to convey the meaning that man is as bad as he possibly can be and that every trace of moral rectitude has been lost in fallen man. 'Total depravity' is intended to indicate that the evil principle . . . has invaded each part of human nature, that there is no part of it which can now invariably perform righteous acts or invariably think righteous thoughts."[4] In other words, man's total depravity means that *every area of his life* is blighted—not that everything about him is *totally bad.* His depravity is also total in that apart from God's grace he is forever lost.

The tragedy of the Fall went far beyond Adam and Eve. It was race-wide in its effect: "Therefore, just as sin entered the world through one man, and death through sin, and in this way death came to all men, because all sinned" (Rom. 5:12).

Men have held to three kinds of appraisals of the effect of the Fall on the human race:

1. The British monk Pelagius said that all men could be sinless if they chose, and that some men have lived free from sin. Pelagius reasoned that since a man can live free from sin, he must have been born into the world free from sin. Consequently, Adam's sin must have affected only Adam. In other words, Pelagius denied "original sin." Carrying his line of thinking further, he asserted that man has no need of supernatural help to live a righteous life. Pelagius did, however, recognize sin's force of habit and its harmful example to others.

2. Augustine, the great bishop of North Africa, rose to do battle with Pelagius' heretical view, and it is with his name that the *second* view of the Fall is connected. Augustine insisted that Adam transmitted to his posterity, because of the unity of the human race, both his guilt and the corruption belonging to it. The nature that man now has, said Augustine, is like the corrupted nature of Adam. Man has lost his freedom not to sin. He is free to carry out the desires of his nature—but since his nature itself is corrupt, he is really free only to do evil. Augustine used the phrase "The will is free, but not freed." Though he has a free choice, man *chooses* a perverse course.

3. Roman Catholics generally hold a halfway position, called semi-Pelagianism—that in the Fall man lost the supernatural gift of righteousness which was not his by nature anyway, but had been added by God. In the Fall, man reverted to his natural state, without this righteousness that God had given him. So he is only *half* sick. Man, according to this view, still

has a special gift of the Spirit which is sufficient to enable him to be righteous if he allows his will to cooperate with God's Spirit.

The Scripture is clear that, though there may be a difference between men in their *degree* of sin, there is no difference in the *fact* of sin (cf. Rom. 3:9-10, 22-23; Isa. 53:6). The whole world is under judgment (Rom. 3:19), and because all men are apart from Christ, they are rebels against God, "children of disobedience" (KJV) subject to His wrath (Eph. 2:2-4).

History and experience bear testimony to the universality of sin. The Augustinian view is closest to the biblical view—that man inherits a tendency to sin which always, to some extent, makes itself manifest. "The Lord saw how great man's wickedness on the earth had become, and that every inclination of the thoughts of his heart was only evil all the time" (Gen. 6:5). When David said, "Surely I was sinful at birth, sinful from the time my mother conceived me" (Ps. 51:5), he was not speaking of the act of conception as sinful, but of the inherited bias to sin that is transmitted at conception.

Anyone who has ever had children recognizes clearly that self-centeredness shows up in the next generation at a very early age. You don't have to teach a child to be selfish. A great deal of effort on the part of Christian parents goes toward trying to overcome this tendency. The only one who has ever escaped this inherited bias toward sin is our Lord Himself.

Adam Our Representative

The Bible clearly teaches that Adam was our representative when he sinned (Rom. 5:12-19). Adam represented us just as, when our government declares war, it represents, affects, and involves us. As a result of Adam's sin, all who are in Adam die. This includes each of us. We tend to think that things might have turned out differently if we had been in Adam's place. But each of us, by doing as Adam did, has ratified the decision our first parents made to rebel and disobey God. Who would claim he had never sinned? And so we are justly condemned today not only for Adam's sin, but for our own sins.

But believers are also represented in Christ. The Bible teaches that, as in Adam all die, so in Christ all believers will be made alive (Rom. 5:19). The glory of the Gospel is that God did something for us in Christ that we could not do for ourselves. Because Adam's original sin is charged to us, we inherit a corrupt nature. Through Christ, the second Adam, we inherit a *new* nature. From Adam we received sin and guilt. From Christ we receive forgiveness and righteousness.

Sin, it is important to realize, does not begin with overt acts, nor is it limited to them. The acts proceed out of a corrupt heart and mind. In other words, we are not sinners because we sin — we sin because we are sinners. An apple tree is not an apple tree because it bears apples; it bears apples because it has the nature of an apple tree. Sins are the acts (or the apples); sin is our corrupt nature (the apple tree).

Through Christ we are not only forgiven our individual acts of sin, but we receive a new nature. The Gospel solution is radical, not merely one of outward reform. Someone has said, "Christ puts a new man in the suit — not just a new suit on the man." When the person is changed by Christ, his clothing (his particular actions) will tend to change as well.

Why We Are Responsible

But how can we be responsible for being sinners if God gave us a hopeless start in life? How can He then condemn us? The answer is twofold. First, as we have seen, we share Adam's sin. But beyond that, God has made full provision, through the sacrifice of Christ, for us to escape judgment. Scripture emphasizes man's ability to receive Christ if he wants to. As Jesus told Nicodemus, "*This* is the verdict: Light has come into the world, but men loved darkness instead of light because their deeds were evil" (John 3:19, italics added). It has been said that the entrance to hell is guarded by a cross. No one comes into hell without walking past it. In other words, at Calvary God did everything necessary to keep man from judgment. If he refuses God's provision, man must himself bear responsibility for judgment.

But isn't it true, many people ask, that men are not all equally bad? Of course this is true. That "all have sinned" does not imply that all are as bad as they might be. But in relation to God's standard of holiness, all come short. You probably know honest, kind, and upright people who are not to be compared with the derelicts of Skid Row or with vicious criminals behind bars. Humanly, there are great differences.

But suppose we were to put one person in Death Valley, 280 feet below sea level; one in Denver, the mile-high city; and one on the peak of Mount Everest, altitude 29,000 feet. Let's suppose that the person in Death Valley represents the dregs of society and the kind of life such people live. The person in Denver is the "average man," and the one on Mount Everest is the best person you can imagine. The enormous differences in their altitude, or elevation, are apparent. But let's suppose God's standard of holiness is represented by the distance to the moon. In this century, we have had an opportunity to see how Mount Everest, Denver, and Death Valley look from the moon. They're all the same!

From our human standpoint, there are great differences in men's sinfulness, but—contrasted with the infinite holiness of God—all men are equally lost.

Sin Is against God

Sin is always primarily directed against God. It is more than mere self-centeredness. David, though he had wronged Bathsheba in adultery, and had murdered Uriah, cried out, "Against You, *You only,* have I sinned and done what is evil in Your sight" (Ps. 51:4, italics added).

The Bible defines sin variously as "transgression of the Law" (1 John 3:4, KJV), as falling short of the mark (Rom. 3:23), and as failure to do the good we know we should do (James 4:17). Sin has both an active, overt aspect (transgression of the Law) and a passive aspect (failure to do good). There are sins of commission and sins of omission. *The Book of Common Prayer* adequately summarizes in its General Confession, "We have done those things we ought not to have done and we have left undone those things we ought to have done."

The first sin was the prototype of all other sins. The seriousness of the first sin lies in the fact that Adam and Eve broke a commandment of God that showed His authority, goodness, wisdom, justice, faithfulness, and grace. In their transgression, they rejected His authority, doubted His goodness, disputed His wisdom, repudiated His justice, contradicted His truthfulness, and spurned His grace. Then and now, sin is the opposite of God's perfection.[5]

The seriousness of sin is based on man's alienation from and broken fellowship with God. It brought disastrous consequences to Adam, and to humanity and society in general. The root problem in the world today is not ignorance or poverty, as great as these are. The root problem is sin. Man is alienated from God, and hence is self-centered. The tensions between racial groups, economic classes, and nations are nothing more than the self-centeredness of the individual blown up on a wide canvas to include all men.

The Good News

If no power is strong enough to change human nature, there is no hope for man. But the good news of the Gospel is that there *is* such power—in Christ. "Where sin increased, grace increased all the more" (Rom. 5:20).

Unless we understand what the Bible teaches about the nature of man in Creation and the devastating effects of the Fall, we cannot understand the grandeur of the grace of God. Many problems in understanding God's grace stem from an inflated view of man and his character and a shrunken view of God and His holiness.

These issues are matters of life and death. Man does not live and die like an animal. Death does not end man's existence. The soul and spirit survive the body. Jesus Himself spoke clearly of this continued existence for both the saved and the lost: "I am the resurrection and the life. He who believes in Me will live even though he dies; and whoever lives and believes in Me will never die" (John 11:25-26). In the story of the rich man and Lazarus (Luke 16:19-31), Christ clearly taught the continued conscious existence of the unjust. The whole teaching of the New Testament about future judgment rests on the assumption that the soul survives after death. "Man is destined to die once, and after that to face judgment" (Heb. 9:27; cf. Rom. 2:5-11; 2 Cor. 5:10).

The Resurrection applies not only to those who will be raised to be with Christ forever (1 Thes. 4:16), but also to the wicked, who will be raised for judgment. Jesus said clearly, "A time is coming when *all* who are in their graves will hear His voice and come out—those who have done *good* will rise to live, and those who have done *evil* will rise to be condemned" (John 5:28-29, italics added).

The sobering truth that we exist forever makes it imperative that we give thought to our nature, condition, and destiny while we are still able to do what is needful.

In answer to the question "Who am I?" the Bible clearly says that each of us is a personality created purposefully by God in His own image. It teaches that we have eternal significance and that our souls are worth more than the whole world (Mark 8:36). God Himself says that He has a plan and a purpose for each life, that we are morally responsible to respond to Him, and that we *can* respond in faith. We have an eternal destiny—either in His presence forever, or in everlasting separation from Him.

The Bible is the most realistic book ever written. It not only describes God as He really is, but us as we really are. It gives us a clear vision of our own nature and destiny, and that of the human race.

CHAPTER SIX

The Holy Spirit

f the three persons in the Godhead—Father, Son, and Holy Spirit—the Holy Spirit seems to be least known and understood today. Yet He is most vitally and intimately involved in our initial conversion and birth into the family of God, as well as in the ongoing development of our Christian lives. Knowledge of and intimate relationship with the Holy Spirit bring us power, joy, and hope. When we neglect Him, through ignorance or indifference, we insure spiritual poverty.

It is of great importance that we be clear in our minds that God the Holy Spirit is as much a *person* as God the Father and God the Son. Many Christians are inclined to speak of Him as an impersonal "it." They give the impression that the Holy Spirit is no more than an influence. Perhaps this is partially due to the fact that we use the term *spirit* in casual conversation in this sense. We speak of the "spirit" of the times or say that "a spirit of expectancy swept the crowd as they awaited the arrival of the President."

Misunderstanding may partially stem also from the fact that the work of the Holy Spirit is not as visibly prominent as that of the Father and of the Son. His work is never to call attention to Himself. Jesus, in speaking of the gift of the Spirit, said, "He will not speak on His own; He will speak only what

The Holy Spirit

He hears, and He will tell you what is yet to come" (John 16:13-14).

Some of the names and symbols by which the Holy Spirit is called may seem to suggest that He is not a personal being. Both the Hebrew and Greek words translated *spirit* mean, basically, "breath" or "wind." The Greek word is in the neuter gender, which is why the *King James Version*—adding to the confusion—translates "the Spirit *itself*" (Rom. 8:16, 26, italics added). The *New International Version* and later versions read "The Spirit Himself."

Impersonal Symbols

Then, too, the symbols used in Scripture to describe the influence of the Spirit include oil, fire, and water—all of which are impersonal. To a superficial student, these symbols could imply that the Spirit is merely an influence. Yet the Father and the Son are described in similar figurative ways—as light, bread of life, living water, etc.

When we speak of the personality of the Holy Spirit, however, we must remind ourselves of the significance of this term as applied to God. As we have observed, God was not made in the image of man, but man in the image of God. *Personality* is not a perfect term for use with God, but it is descriptive of the Spirit's nature. It is comforting to know that the Holy Spirit has a mind, feelings, and a will, as God the Father does. He is a *person* in this sense.

It is impossible to explain many biblical references to the Holy Spirit apart from the fact that He is equal in His personal nature to the Father and the Son.

Jesus gave some of the clearest scriptural teaching about the Holy Spirit. He called the Spirit the Comforter (kjv), or Counselor (niv), "whom the Father will send in My name, [to] teach you all things and [to] remind you of everything I have said to you" (John 14:26). These titles clearly imply personality. The terms *Comforter* or *Counselor* convey the idea of a person, such as a lawyer, on whom a believer calls for help. Obviously, counseling and comforting would not be possible if the Spirit were merely an impersonal influence.

In John 16:7, as in the previous reference, the emphasis is on Christ's going away and the Holy Spirit's being sent by the Father to replace our Lord Himself. This change, Jesus said, would be beneficial for His disciples. An impersonal force could hardly improve on the personal presence of Jesus Christ.

Repeatedly (John 16:7-15), Jesus used the masculine personal pronoun *He* when referring to the Spirit. As we have pointed out, the Greek word translated *spirit* is the same as that for *breath*, and is neuter in gender. Jesus used the masculine pronoun deliberately, intending it to indicate personality and intimacy.

Though the Holy Spirit is not mentioned with the Father and the Son in New Testament greetings and salutations (e.g., 1 Cor. 1:3; Gal. 1:3; etc.), He is mentioned in the baptismal formula. The Lord told the disciples, "Therefore go and make disciples of all nations, baptizing them in the name of the Father and of the Son and of the Holy Spirit" (Matt. 28:19). The Spirit is also included in the Pauline benediction, "May the grace of the Lord Jesus Christ, and the love of God, and the fellowship of the Holy Spirit be with you all" (2 Cor. 13:14). Association of the Holy Spirit with the other two Persons of the Trinity also appears in 1 Peter 1:1-2 and in Jude 20-21.

We can *treat* the Spirit as a *person*. Ananias was struck dead for lying to the Holy Spirit (Acts 5:3). The Spirit may be *grieved* (Eph. 4:30) and *sinned against* by unforgivable blasphemy (Mark 3:29). None of these things would be true of an impersonal force.

The Holy Spirit *does* things which only a person could do. He *speaks:* "The Spirit told Phillip, 'Go to that chariot and stay near it' " (Acts 8:29). He *strives:* "My Spirit will not contend with man forever" (Gen. 6:3). "The Spirit also helps our infirmities. . . and *makes intercession* for us" (Rom. 8:26, italics added). He *reveals, searches,* and *knows:* "God has revealed it to us by His Spirit. The Spirit searches all things, even the deep things of God. . . . No one knows the thoughts of God except the Spirit of God" (1 Cor. 2:10-11). He distributes spiritual gifts "to each one, just as He [the Spirit] determines" (1 Cor. 12:11). None of these verbs could rightly be used of a mere influence.

Identified with Believers

The Holy Spirit is identified with the thinking of believers. At the Council of Jerusalem the disciples declared, "It seemed good to us *and* to the Holy Spirit" (cf. Acts 15:28).

The Holy Spirit is not only a person—He is Deity. He is specifically called "God" in the Ananias incident (Acts 5:4). Paul says, "Now the Lord is the Spirit" (2 Cor. 3:17; cf. v. 18), and again,"Don't you know that you yourselves are God's temple and . . . that God's Spirit dwells in you?" (1 Cor. 3:16)

Our Lord says that blasphemy against the Holy Spirit is worse than blasphemy against the Son of man. This can only mean that blasphemy against the Spirit maligns and discredits God.

The Holy Spirit possesses attributes which belong only to Deity. He is *eternal:* "Christ, who through the eternal Spirit offered Himself" (Heb. 9:14). He is *omnipresent:* "Where can I go from Your Spirit? Where can I flee from Your presence?" (Ps. 139:7) He is the "Spirit of *life"* (Rom. 8:2, italics added) and the "Spirit of *truth"* (John 16:13, italics added).

The Spirit does God's work. He was involved in *Creation:* "The Spirit of God moved upon the . . . waters" (Gen. 1:2, KJV). He is involved in *regeneration,* the new birth: "So it is with everyone born of the Spirit" (John 3:8). Jesus cast out demons by the Spirit: "I drive out demons by the Spirit of God" (Matt. 12:28). The Holy Spirit participates in *resurrection:* "And if the Spirit of Him who raised Jesus from the dead is living in you, He . . . will also give life to your mortal bodies through His Spirit, who lives in you" (Rom. 8:11).

The New Testament quotes many Old Testament passages in which the speaker is Jehovah, the Lord. In the New Testament, such messages are often attributed to the Holy Spirit. For instance, Isaiah said, "I heard the voice of the Lord" (Isa.

6:8). But Paul said, "The *Holy Spirit* spoke the truth to your forefathers when He said through Isaiah the prophet . . . 'You will be ever hearing but never understanding' " (Acts 28:25-26, italics added).

Just as the truth of the Trinity is hinted at in the Old Testament but awaits its fullest expression in the New, so with truth about the Holy Spirit. His personality and Deity are evident in the Old Testament, but the full expression of His activity is given only in the New Testament. There is no conflict here with the Old Testament, but the New Testament picture is much more complete.

Old Testament Teaching

Five differing aspects of the work of the Spirit are discernible in the Old Testament:[1]

1. The work of the Spirit in the creation of the universe (Gen. 1:2) and of man. "The Spirit of God has made me; the breath of the Almighty gives me life" (Job 33:4).

2. The work of the Spirit in equipping for service. He conferred power on judges and warriors. For instance, "The Spirit of the Lord came mightily upon [Samson]" (Jud. 14:6). The Israelites cried out to God and He gave them Othniel, "and the Spirit of the Lord came upon him, so that he became Israel's judge and went to war" (Jud. 3:10). When the Spirit came upon people for a particular purpose in this manner, He did not necessarily transform their moral character.

Wisdom and skill for particular jobs, including those of a nonspiritual nature, were imparted to various individuals by the Spirit. Bezaleel was filled with the Spirit to work in gold, silver, and brass for the tabernacle (Ex. 31:2-5)

3. The work of the Spirit in inspiring the prophets. Usually they began their message with, "This is what the Lord says." At times, however, they also attributed their message to the Holy Spirit: "The Spirit came into me and raised me to my feet, and I heard Him speaking to me" (Ezek. 2:2). And Moses exclaimed, "Are you jealous for *my* sake? I wish that all the Lord's people were prophets, and that the Lord would put His

Spirit on them!" (Num. 11:29, italics added)

4. The work of the Holy Spirit in producing moral living. David, in agony of repentance for his dual sin of adultery and murder, pleaded for God to create a clean heart in him, and begged, "Take not Thy Holy Spirit from me" (Ps. 51:11, KJV). The Spirit, David knew, is good, and He leads men to do God's will (Ps. 143:10; cf. 139:23-24).

5. The work of the Spirit in foretelling the coming of the Messiah. The references which anticipate Christ are of two kinds. First are those which prophesy a direct indwelling of the Spirit in one messianic figure: "The Spirit of the Sovereign Lord is on Me, because the Lord has anointed Me to preach good news" (Isa. 61:1). Jesus, early in His ministry, read this passage in the synagogue at Nazareth and concluded with the electrifying words, "Today this Scripture is fulfilled in your hearing" (Luke 4:18-21; Isa. 9:2-9; 42:1-4).

The second way the Holy Spirit anticipated Christ was in the more general way of speaking about the new covenant people of God. "I will give you a new heart and put a new spirit in you" (Ezek. 36:26; cf. v. 27). Both this prophecy and the comprehensive promise to Joel speak of the Spirit being given to all classes: "And . . . I will pour out My Spirit on all people" (Joel 2:28; cf. v. 29).

Equips for a Task

The Old Testament's earlier teaching on the Holy Spirit emphasized the coming of the Spirit to equip a person to perform a certain task. The Scripture suggests that out of this bestowal of the Spirit, men grew more conscious of their inner need for God's help if they were to be morally pure enough to serve the Lord. Later in the Old Testament period, some scholars detect an awareness, on the part of believers, that the human government of Israel would never succeed in achieving the purposes of Jehovah, and a growing realization that, in time, the Spirit would be given to all God's people.[2]

Glimpses of the person and work of the Holy Spirit in the Old Testament are numerous and clear. However, the Old

Testament period could not be called "the age of the Spirit" as our age is called, since the coming of the Holy Spirit in fullness on the Day of Pentecost had not yet occurred. Before Pentecost the Spirit came on particular people for particular tasks. While men could have an intimate relationship with Him, as shown by David's experience, the fellowship was not as personal or as permanent as is possible since Pentecost. The Spirit came upon individuals temporarily and then, when the occasion for His coming was over, withdrew. Samson's tragic downfall resulted from the Spirit's withdrawal. Samson had become so insensitive that he was not even aware that the Spirit had left him (Jud. 16:20). Nor was the experience of the Spirit in that era as widespread or universal as it is now, when He indwells everyone who is in the church of Jesus Christ by the new birth. It is emphatically true that "if anyone does not have the Spirit of Christ, he does not belong to Christ" (Rom. 8:9).

Our Lord's words to the disciples in this connection are instructive: "[The Spirit] lives *with* you and will be *in* you" (John 14:17, italics added). Just as there was a dispute over the Trinity in the church during the Arian controversy, and at the same time a question as to whether the Son of God had existed eternally or was the first of God's creatures, so there was also conflict concerning the Holy Spirit. In the Nicene Creed He is called, "The Lord, the Life-Giver, that proceeds from the Father, that with the Father and Son is together worshiped and together glorified." This formula was finally adopted by the Council of Chalcedon in A.D. 451.

"Procession" and "Generation"

The phrase "proceeds from the Father" is taken from the Gospel of John: "When the Counselor comes, whom I will send to you from the Father. . . . He will testify about Me" (15:26). This statement and others (e.g., John 16:7; 14:16; 20:22; etc.) imply a type of subordination of the Spirit to the Father and Son. This is only a subordination of relationship, not of deity.

Neither "generation" nor "procession" indicate a lack of equality within the Godhead, nor do they imply a creation or beginning of existence. Rather, they imply an eternal relation to the Father. They are "not a relation in any way analogous to physical derivation, but a life-movement of the divine nature, in virtue of which Father, Son, and Holy Spirit, while equal in essence and dignity, stand to each other in order of personality, office, and operation, and in virtue of which the Father works through the Son, and the Father and Son through the Spirit."[3]

In the year A.D. 589 the words *and from the Son* were added to the Nicene Creed. This addition created tremendous controversy. The Western church insisted on the addition to insure the preservation of the scriptural teaching that the Holy Spirit is the Spirit of Christ as well as of the Father. The Eastern church refuses this insertion, believing it weakens the doctrine of subordination and makes our Lord a separate source of deity. But "the union of the Father and the Son in 'sending' the Spirit really works against any idea of differentiation which would mar the inner harmony of the divine Triad. . . . Scripture seems clearly to state that while the Spirit proceeds from the Father, He was also 'given' by the Son to His church, and that He is as much the Spirit of Christ as the Spirit of God."[4]

Some of the references that clarify the concepts of the Spirit's Deity and personality are: "God's Spirit lives in you" (1 Cor. 3:16); "the Spirit of Christ" (Rom. 8:9); and "God sent the Spirit of His Son into our hearts" (Gal. 4:6).

His Other Titles

Other descriptive titles of the Holy Spirit include "the Spirit of grace" (Heb. 10:29); "the Spirit of truth" (cf. 1 John 5:6); "the Spirit of wisdom and understanding, the Spirit of counsel and power, the Spirit of knowledge and of the fear of the Lord" (Isa. 11:2). He is the "Spirit of promise," that is, the One who came in fulfillment of Christ's promise (Eph. 1:13, KJV). He is also "the Spirit of glory" (1 Peter 4:14).

The Holy Spirit, then, is completely personal and completely God. He is coequal and coeternal with the Father and the Son.

We have already seen glimpses of the Spirit's work. We shall now look at it more closely. Though the Holy Spirit is self-effacing, His is the direct work of God and vitally affects each of us as individuals. He is active at various levels. In general, the Holy Spirit functions as the Executor of the purposes and plans of the Godhead. He is the One who carries out God's purposes—creation, conviction, regeneration, enlightenment, sanctification, and glorification.

In relationship to the world, the Spirit took part in the creation of the universe, as already mentioned in our review of His Old Testament activities. He is also referred to as the Preserver of nature: "When You send Your Spirit, they [the fish] are created, and You renew the face of the earth" (Ps. 104:30).

Jesus outlined the work of the Spirit so far as humanity as a whole is concerned. He convicts the world of sin, of righteousness, and of judgment (John 16:8-11). As we saw in chapter 1, the Holy Spirit is the Author of the Scriptures, the One who inspired them (2 Peter 1:20-21). He is also the One who interprets them and applies them to our hearts at a particular time. He is the Spirit of wisdom and revelation (Eph. 1:17), and He interprets the mind of God (1 Cor. 2:9-14). It has been rightly observed that this "illuminating" work of the Holy Spirit never becomes so mystical and subjective that grammatical and historical consistency are abandoned. By misunderstanding the role of the Holy Spirit in interpreting the Word, some have made the Bible almost a magical book, equating their subjective feelings with the authority of the Spirit.

The Spirit and Christ

The Holy Spirit had a particularly intimate relationship with the Lord Jesus Christ, who in His humanity was completely dependent on the Spirit. He was *conceived* by the Holy Spirit and *born* of Him (Luke 1:35). Jesus was *led* by the Spirit (Matt. 4:1). He was *anointed* for His ministry by the Spirit in a special way at His baptism (Matt. 3:13-17). He *offered* Himself as a sacrifice through the Spirit (Heb. 9:14), and He was *raised* from the dead by the power of the Spirit (Rom. 1:4). He gave *commandments* to the apostles, and through them to the church by the Spirit (Acts 1:2).

In the church, the Holy Spirit administers spiritual gifts for the good of the whole body: "The manifestation of the Spirit is given for the common good" (1 Cor. 12:7; cf. entire chapter). He is the dynamic power which was promised the church before Pentecost: "You will receive power when the Holy Spirit comes on you" (Acts 1:8). Because of the phenomenal exploits of the early church, which turned the Roman world upside down, the Book of Acts has been called by some "the Acts of the Holy Spirit."

Through the work of the Holy Spirit in the individual Christian, a believer comes into the most intimate personal contact with God.

The Holy Spirit is the One who brings conviction of sin to an individual (John 16:8). Whenever a person comes to a sense of his own sinfulness, whether by the preached, written, or personally spoken word, the Spirit of God has been at work.

The Spirit's Sealing

As soon as a person puts his trust in Christ, he is "sealed" by the Holy Spirit (Eph. 1:13). A seal is a symbol of a finished transaction, of ownership, and of security. Because we are sealed by the Spirit, we can have certainty and assurance of salvation: "The Spirit Himself testifies with our spirit that we are God's children" (Rom. 8:16).

The Spirit indwells each individual Christian, whose body is the Spirit's temple. Along with the Incarnation and Resurrection, here is another indication from Scripture that the human body is not inherently evil or sinful. It also reminds us that we are to take our bodies seriously. They are never to be in any way mutilated, abused, or neglected. Scripture is against the kind of asceticism which punishes the body in the interests of "spirituality." Extreme forms of such self-affliction occurred at different periods of church history, particularly in medieval times, and more sophisticated forms are with us even today.

We are sealed and indwelt by the Holy Spirit at the time we are baptized by the Spirit, "for we were all baptized by one Spirit into one body—whether Jews or Greeks, slave or free—and we were all given the one Spirit to drink" (1 Cor. 12:13). This baptism, with its attendant sealing and indwelling by the Spirit, takes place at the time of conversion. This participation in the Spirit is shared by all believers, despite their varying degrees of maturity, strength, and devotion.

Some Christians, however, apply the term *baptism* to one's first experience of being *filled* with the Spirit, which experience is part of God's purpose for us (Eph. 5:18).

No one is a Christian who does not have the Holy Spirit (Rom. 8:9), for He indwells and seals *every* believer. Unfortunately, many Christians never know the joy and power of the Holy Spirit's fullness.

Filled with the Spirit

This being filled with the Spirit is not a once-for-all experience, but one that may be repeated. On the Day of Pentecost the disciples were filled with the Spirit (Acts 2:4). A few days later, in a dramatic prayer meeting, they had such an experience again (Acts 4:31).

The filling of the Spirit implies being given power and boldness for God's service, and strength to meet particular crises. It is possible, and it sometimes happens, that the baptism of the Spirit and the infilling of the Spirit take place at the same time. They need not be separated in experience. But the filling of the Spirit is an experience to be repeated as necessary in the life of each believer. We are, literally, to "keep on being filled" (cf. Eph. 5:18).

The Holy Spirit is not a substance, but a Person. The fullness of the Spirit is not a matter of our receiving more of Him. Rather, it is a matter of relationship. To be filled with the Spirit means we allow Him to occupy, guide, and control every area of our lives. His power can then work through us, making us effectively fruitful for God and flooding our hearts with His joy. This filling applies not only to our outward acts but to our inner thoughts and motives. When we are filled with the Spirit, all we are and have is subject to His control.

The test as to whether or not you are filled with the Spirit is not, "Have you received an external sign or been given a particular gift of the Spirit?" Rather, "Have you given yourself wholly and without reservation to God?" (Rom. 12:1) Are you genuinely willing that He should control, absolutely and entirely, your life? Many believers come to a point of utter frustration in their service for the Lord simply because they fail to realize the need to be filled with the Spirit if they are to act in God's power. Just as we cannot *save* ourselves apart from the work of the Holy Spirit, neither can we *live* the life of victory or serve the Lord effectively without the Spirit. When we learn to trust Him fully, allowing Him to work through us, we are freed from the frustration of trying to accomplish spiritual and eternal results solely through our human ability—or, more properly, inability.

It is the Holy Spirit who delivers us from the power of sin: "Through Christ Jesus the law of the Spirit of life set me free from the law of sin and death" (Rom. 8:2). The Holy Spirit changes the *pattern* of our lives so that we *can* overcome sin. He does not make us sinless (1 John 1:8), but in Him we are able to start fulfilling the righteousness of the Law (Rom. 8:4). Such holy living is a work of the Spirit and a *result* of salvation; it is not in any way the *basis* for our being saved.

The Spirit's Fruit

When the Holy Spirit produces His fruit in us, we find that "love, joy, peace, patience, kindness, goodness, faithfulness, gentleness, and self-control" (cf. Gal. 5:22-23) come naturally to us instead of our having to labor strenuously to cultivate these traits.

The Holy Spirit is also a guide to the individual Christian. We are instructed to "walk in the Spirit" (Gal. 5:16). His leadership is one of the signs that an individual is really a child of God: "Those who are led by the Spirit of God, are sons of God" (Rom. 8:14). The Holy Spirit clearly led and guided the early Christians, as we read in the Book of Acts, and He does the same today if a Christian is open and sensitive to His control.

The Holy Spirit prays for us (Rom. 8:26). What a wonderful thing to realize, especially when we don't know how to pray, that the Spirit of God makes intercession for us!

The opposite of this intimate, loving, dynamic relationship with the Holy Spirit is experienced when we offend Him. We are not to "grieve" the Spirit (Eph. 4:30). To grieve is to make sad. In the verses immediately following this command, some of the things that grieve the Spirit are enumerated. They have to do with attitudes, thoughts, words, and actions. Other things also grieve God's Spirit—idolatry, hatred, jealousy, fits of rage, selfish ambition, envy, etc. (Gal. 5:18-21). To withhold anything from Him is to grieve Him. It is a solemn thing to realize that even as *we* can be grieved, we can also, in a much more profound way, grieve God's Holy Spirit.

We are commanded, "Quench not the Spirit" (1 Thes. 5:19, KJV). The *New International Version* renders it, "Do not put out the Spirit's fire." Because the figure of quenching suggests the idea of fire, some believe that this sin is more related to outward service than to motives and attitudes. In the scriptural context it suggests both. The verse follows a call to rejoice, pray, and give thanks. It precedes a warning not to despise whatever claims to be of God, but to test it. We may not only quench the Spirit in ourselves, but by sinful living, confused beliefs, and unconcern quench His work in and for others as well. On the other hand, the Spirit may well use others to correct, enlighten, and encourage *us*. To fail to receive God's Word through another person simply because he, like us, is imperfect, is to quench God's own Holy Spirit.

Through the Holy Spirit we *come* to know Christ, and by the Holy Spirit's power we *live* and *grow* in Christ, in the service of the King and in the fellowship of His church.

CHAPTER SEVEN

The Church

great many ecclesiastical leaders today are admittedly uncertain as to just what the church is. One modern theologian has written a book whose title sums up what is in the minds of many people: *The Misunderstanding of the Church*. Small wonder, then, that confusion about the church is common in the minds of "ordinary" Christians, especially in view of the increasing extent to which "the church" is in the news. The ecumenical movement is increasingly influential, and denominational mergers are occurring with more frequency than had been thought possible.

Among (and sometimes even *within*) the various groups of "Christians," there is considerable difference of opinion about matters of form, church government, mode of baptism, essential doctrines, etc. Some competing groups profess to be "the *one* 'true' church." It is especially important, in view of all the conflicting voices heard today, that every Christian knows what the Bible teaches about the church.

In the New Testament, the Greek word *ekklēsia*, translated "church," means a "called out" group, or "assembly"—not necessarily a religious one. The Ephesus town clerk, trying to quell a near riot, said, "If there is anything further you want to bring up, it must be settled in a legal assembly [*ekklēsia*]" (Acts 19:39).

Applied to Christians, *the church* means "those who have been called out to Jesus Christ." In the New Testament, according to D.W.B. Robinson, it "mostly means a local congregation of Christians, and never a building. . . . Although we often speak of these congregations collectively as the New Testament church, or the early church, no New Testament writer uses *ekklēsia* in this collective way. Its commonest use was for the public assembly of citizens duly summoned, which was a feature of all the cities outside Judea where the Gospel was planted."[1] The term also applied to the universal church, the body of Christ: "God placed all things under His [Christ's] feet and appointed Him to be head over everything for the *church*, which is His body" (Eph. 1:22-23, italics added).

The New Testament church, then, is defined in two ways. First, it is "the whole company of regenerate persons . . . in heaven and on earth" (cf. Matt. 16:18; Eph. 5:24-25; Heb. 12:23).[2] This is the universal invisible church. It is universal in that it includes all true believers in every place, and those who have gone on as well as those still alive. It is invisible in that it is not apparent in its entirety at any given time or place.

Second, there is also the individual local group, or church, through which the universal church is evident. Strong writes, "The individual church may be defined as that smaller company of regenerate persons who, in any given community, unite themselves voluntarily together in accordance with Christ's laws, for the purpose of securing the complete establishment of His kingdom in themselves and in the world."[3]

People in View

In both definitions, *people* are in view—not buildings. Today we use the word *church* in several additional ways. In answer to the question, "Where is your church?" we are more likely to answer, "At 18th and Green Streets" than "At County Hospital," "Joe's Texaco Station," "Motorola," or "Circle Campus." Really a church is where its members are at any given time. Part of our problem, in reaching the world today, results from our "building" mentality. When we think of the activities of the church, we tend to think only of what goes on within the four walls of the church building, rather than what takes place *in the world* through what believers say, do, and *are*.

God has always had His people. From the time of the Fall, when God gave Adam and Eve His promise of the Redeemer (Gen. 3:15), all who have believed His promises have been His people. God called Abraham and promised him, "I will bless those who bless you, and whoever curses you I will curse; and all peoples on earth will be blessed through you" (Gen. 12:3). He established an eternal covenant with the nation of Israel as His "chosen people." They were not chosen because of inherent superiority over other racial or ethnic groups. "The Lord did not set His affection on you and choose you because you were more numerous than other peoples, for you were the fewest of all peoples. But it was because the Lord loved you and kept the oath He swore to your forefathers" (Deut. 7:7-8).

Merely being born into the nation of Israel did not make a person one of God's people spiritually: "A man is not a Jew if he is only one outwardly, nor is circumcision merely outward and physical. No, a man is a Jew if he is one inwardly; and circumcision is circumcision of the heart, by the Spirit, not by the written code" (Rom. 2:28-29). Many who were not Jews physically became Jews spiritually by recognizing Jehovah as the true and living God and turning from idols to Him. Perhaps the most dramatic example of conversion to Judaism was in the days of Esther, after the Jews' deliverance from Haman. "In every province and in every city, wherever the edict of the king went, there was joy and gladness among the Jews, with feasting and celebrating. And many people of other nationalities became Jews" (Es. 8:17). The occasion is still celebrated today in the Feast of Purim.

Members of the church are to have an intimate relationship with each other as well as to Christ. Therefore what hurts one member will hurt all, and when one member is honored, all the others will rejoice with him (cf. 1 Cor. 12:26).

The church was first mentioned by Jesus: "On this rock I will build My church, and the gates of Hades will not overcome it" (Matt. 16:18). On another occasion He described the simplest form of a church, saying, "For where two or three come together in My name, there am I with them" (Matt. 18:20).

Began at Pentecost

The Christian church, as such, came into being with the coming of the Holy Spirit on the Day of Pentecost. After Peter's sermon on that occasion, "Those who accepted his message were baptized, and about three thousand were added to their number that day. They devoted themselves to the apostles' teaching and to the fellowship, to the breaking of bread and to prayer. . . . And the Lord added to their number daily those who were being saved" (Acts 2:41-42, 47). The church was born in Jerusalem. It at first consisted mainly of Jews who recognized Jesus as the Messiah. Many of them were Hellenists—that is, Greek-speaking Jews—who had been scattered all over the empire. Many came to Jerusalem regularly as pilgrims.

The church was at first considered a sect within Judaism. One of Paul's accusers referred to him as "a troublemaker, stirring up riots among the Jews all over the world. He is a ringleader of the Nazarene sect" (Acts 24:5). The Roman government gave Christians the same exemption from military service it gave the Jews. The first Jewish Christians in Jerusalem continued to recognize their obligations to the Mosaic Law and still participated in the worship services of the temple or synagogue.

Increasingly, however, Jewish proselytes (Gentiles who had embraced Judaism) believed the Gospel and came into the church. Philip preached the Good News in Samaria and later baptized an Ethiopian to whom he had witnessed (Acts 8). Only after a vision from the Lord did the universal scope of the Gospel finally get through to reluctant Peter (Acts 10:9-16). He later explained to Cornelius, a Gentile, that it had been "against our law for a Jew to associate with a Gentile or visit him. But God has shown me that I should not call any man impure or unclean" (v. 28).

The Church

On hearing Cornelius' declaration of faith, Peter uttered the historic words, "I now realize how true it is that God does not show favoritism but accepts men from every nation who fear Him and do what is right" (vv. 34-35). As if to vouch for the truth of what Peter was saying, the Holy Spirit came on his listeners, most of whom were Gentiles, as he spoke. The Jews with Peter were amazed that Gentiles also received the Holy Spirit, but Peter baptized them.

Other Christian Jews preached the Gospel in Antioch, where a mixed church of Jews and Gentiles came into existence (Acts 13:1). It was here that believers were first called Christians (Acts 11:26), or "Christ's men."

What relationship Gentile converts should have to the Law and circumcision was the first great question the early church had to decide. A council held in Jerusalem made the momentous declaration, "It seemed good to the Holy Spirit and to us not to burden you with anything beyond the following requirements: You are to abstain from food sacrificed to idols, from blood, from the meat of strangled animals, and from sexual immorality. You will do well to avoid these things" (Acts 15:28-29).

New Testament Figures

The figures used in the New Testament to describe the church are instructive. One is the "body of Christ." Christ is the head of the body. Every member functions under His leadership and in dependence on each other member. "The body is a unit, though it is made up of many parts; and though all its parts are many, they form one body. So it is with Christ" (1 Cor. 12:12; cf. Eph. 4:4; Col. 3:15).

Christ leads the church, and it is to be subject to Him (Eph. 5:23-24). He is the source of its unity—"for you are all one in Christ Jesus" (Gal. 3:28).

The church is also compared to a building: "You also, like living stones, are being built into a spiritual house to be a holy priesthood" (1 Peter 2:5). This household of God is "built upon the foundation of the apostles and prophets, Jesus Christ

Himself being the chief Cornerstone" (Eph. 2:20). This building, or temple, is the dwelling place of the Holy Spirit; it is comprised of all individuals indwelt by the Holy Spirit (1 Cor. 6:19 ff). God Himself dwells within the church, so whoever attacks the church attacks God. In criticizing the church, we must be careful we are not criticizing God.

The Church is called the bride of Christ. Marriage illustrates Christ's relationship to the church (Eph. 5:25-27, 31-32; cf. 2 Cor. 11:2; Rev. 19:7; 22:17). This figure powerfully displays Christ's intense love for His church and His total commitment to her.

The church in the New Testament apparently was relatively simple. There were no denominations, though Paul rebuked party spirit among the Christians in Corinth (1 Cor. 3:3-8). How, then, have we come to the complex situation in which we find the church today?

There are, of course, numerous historical reasons, such as persecutions, heresy, and formation of national churches. But part of the reason for the development of differing groups of believers is the fact that the New Testament gives only limited instruction about church organization and practice. Sincere Christians, all claiming scriptural authority, have always differed in the interpretation of certain passages and teachings of the New Testament. It is important, therefore, to trace the discernible lines of the New Testament church pattern and to understand some of the major interpretations of them.

Membership Requirements

Requirements for church membership are implicit in the Book of Acts. The first was belief in the Lord Jesus Christ (Acts 2:38). Faith in Christ, which normally includes repentance for sin, is the spiritual prerequisite to new life and membership in the body of Christ. When people asked Jesus the question, "What must we do to do the works God requires?" He answered, "The work of God is this: to believe in the one He has sent" (John 6:28-29).

Baptism was to follow faith, as an open confession of trust in

Christ, though some earnest Christians believe that the "one baptism" (Eph. 4:5) is the baptism of the Holy Spirit, and that water baptism is not God's purpose for Christians today.

Adherence to revealed truth, among early Christians, was the standard: "They devoted themselves to the apostles' teaching and to the fellowship, to the breaking of bread and to prayer" (Acts 2:42). Paul warns of false teachers arising within the church (Phil. 3:2), and Peter echoes the same solemn theme. Throughout the New Testament there is emphasis on doctrinal purity and holiness of life. Doctrinal and moral impurity are to be purged from the church (1 Cor. 5:7).

God's "called out" people were designated "saints" (Eph. 1:1; 1 Cor. 1:2; Phil. 1:1). They met together for worship and mutual upbuilding of spiritual life (1 Cor. 14:3, 5, 19; Col. 3:16). The church was an evangelizing fellowship whose purpose was the communication and preservation of the Gospel message throughout the whole world (Matt. 28:19-20; Acts 1:8). Paul's letters placed little stress on evangelism, possibly because early believers were naturally and effectively evangelistic. He wrote to the Thessalonians, "The Lord's message rang out from you not only in Macedonia and Achaia—your faith in God has become known everywhere. Therefore we do not need to say anything about it" (1 Thes. 1:8).

Christians were to be servants, meeting the physical and spiritual needs of both believers and unbelievers. "As we have opportunity, let us do good to all people, especially to those who belong to the family of believers" (Gal. 6:10). Christ Himself was the example; He "went around doing good" (Acts 10:38).

As Leon Morris puts it, "During the history of the church there have been many variations from the New Testament pattern. Indeed, there are so many gaps in our knowledge of what went on in New Testament times that we cannot be quite sure what constituted that pattern. Even those groups who claim to model their polity exactly on the New Testament cannot be certain they have succeeded. . . . No attempt seems to have been made to fasten any pattern on succeeding generations, for no authoritative directions were given as to the mode and perpetuation of the ministry. Ministerial forms have evolved in a variety of ways."[4]

That there was some organization at the local level in New Testament times seems clear. There were stated meetings (Acts 20:7); elected deacons (Acts 6:5-6); membership discipline (1 Cor. 5:13); letters of commendation (Acts 18:27); and lists of widows for support (1 Tim. 5:9).

God gave spiritual gifts to the church. "He gave some to be apostles, some to be prophets, some to be evangelists, and some to be pastors and teachers, to prepare God's people for works of service, so that the body of Christ may be built up" (Eph. 4:11-12). The purpose of these gifts is "for works of service." There is no clear distinction between clergy and laity, either in terms of church government or spiritual ministry.

Periods of Ministry

Hammond outlines the three periods in the New Testament ministry as follows:

1. *The first period.* (a) Our Lord's ministry with the seventy whom He commissioned; (b) the apostolic ministry of those who had specially delegated authority from the Lord to give authoritative leadership in the church after Pentecost; and (c) the ministry of deacons, elders, and bishops. The three pastoral epistles (1 and 2 Tim.; Titus) give the principles of and qualifications for the ministry.

2. *The transitional period.* During most of the lifetime of the apostles, and until the New Testament had been circulated to the various Christian communities, there were special gifts, such as prophecy, in the church. The object of these was to enable the local community to receive the New Testament revelation of Christ direct from the Spirit of God. When the apostles had completed their work, some of these "gifts" ceased. For instance, there was not an unending succession of apostles and prophets (cf. Eph. 2:20; 3:5; 4:11).

3. *The permanent ministry.* A bishop, or elder, was to teach spiritual truth and exercise rule and discipline in the local church. "Remember your leaders, who spoke the word of God

to you. Consider the outcome of their way of life and imitate their faith" (Heb. 13:7; cf. 1 Tim. 5:17).[5]

Deacons helped in administering the business of a church (Acts 6:1-6; 1 Tim. 3:8-12), though it is clear there are spiritual overtones to their activity.

In view of the many denominations and sects throughout church history, it is surprising that all forms of church government and views of the ministry fall generally into one of three groupings: the episcopal, the presbyterial, or the congregational.[6] (These terms, as here used, refer to systems of church government rather than to denominations.)

Episcopalianism

In the episcopalian system, the church is governed by bishops, but there are also presbyters (or priests) and deacons. The only one in this system who has power to ordain is the bishop. The bishops trace their office back many centuries. Some, in fact, claim to trace the line back to the apostles—hence the term so often used: "apostolic succession." Among other groups, the Roman Catholic, Orthodox, Anglican, Episcopal, Methodist, and some Lutheran churches have the episcopal form of government.

This system is actually not found in the New Testament. A full episcopalian system had not yet developed. Those who hold to this type of church government, however, feel that it was a natural development in the second-century church. They see, in the work of some New Testament figures, a transition between the itinerant ministry of the apostles and the more settled ministry of the later bishops. Timothy and Titus had a good deal of authority over a number of churches, yet lacked the wide apostolic authority of Paul. James of Jerusalem is, some believe, an example of an apostle who had a localized ministry but was more like a later bishop than like Paul. The development of episcopacy is traced through the early church fathers.

It is significant, many feel, that there is no trace of a struggle to establish the episcopalian system. If a divinely established presbyterial or congregational system had been overthrown, it is argued, a bitter conflict between the two factions would have been inevitable. By the second century, however, without any such conflict, the episcopal system predominated throughout the whole church.

Presbyterianism

In presbyterianism, the church is governed by elders. Presbyterians recognize that in the New Testament the terms *elder* and *bishop* are used interchangeably and that they are clearly the most important element in the local ministry. In each local church, it would seem, a number of elders formed a kind of committee to handle church affairs. Elders in New Testament times acted with the apostles (Acts 15)—an indication of their importance. When the apostles passed from the scene, elders were the leading officers.

The local congregation seems also to have had a voice in the selection of men for the ministry. They chose the seven deacons (Acts 6:1-6) and apparently had a hand in setting aside Paul and Barnabas for missionary work (Acts 13:1-3). Presbyterians believe in the equality of elders, in the right of the people to take part (through their representatives) in the government of a church, and in the unity of the church through a graduated series of church courts which express and exercise the common authority of the church as a divine society.

John Dall distinguishes presbyterianism from the other two systems as follows: "As opposed to prelacy, the presbyterial type of government rests upon the equality of ministerial status and seeks to give ecclesiastical power to the members of the church instead of to clerical individuals or councils; as opposed to congregationalism, it seeks to realize the unity of the church by entrusting to a carefully devised system of graded church courts legislative, executive, and judicial—not merely advisory—powers."[7]

Presbyterians usually make a distinction between teaching and ruling elders (1 Tim. 5:17). The teaching elder is the principal minister, ordained by the "laying on of the hands" of other elders. This is, in the presbyterial view, ordination to the universal church, not to some small part of it.

Ruling elders are chosen by the congregation and admitted to their office by ordination. They may not preach, baptize, or administer Communion, but they assist in the government of the church and in the exercise of discipline. They also have responsibility for the financial affairs of the church. Some presbyterians feel that the office of ruling elder is the same as that of teaching elder, but others regard ruling elders as laymen.

Presbyterians account for the development of a universal episcopal system by saying that "monarchial" bishops gained the supremacy over presbyters in the church just after the Apostolic Age. They explain that church problems involving persecution and heresy could more easily be met by such a central authority. But this development, presbyterians maintain, was not in harmony with the essential nature of the ministry as revealed in the New Testament. They also believe that their system preserves the "episcopacy" through its "moderators" and general assembly, and that this preservation is not at the expense of ministerial equality.

Congregationalism

The third basic form of church government is congregationalism. Every group whose emphasis is on the autonomy of the local congregation would be included here. Such groups include Baptists, the Open Brethren, Christians (Disciples), Evangelical Free Churches, and some Bible and other independent churches. Followers of this polity hold that no man or group of men should exercise authority over a local congregation of Christ's church. With some exceptions, these churches have two types of ministers—pastors and deacons. Pastors have oversight of the congregation. They are usually ordained or set apart in a service attended by representatives of other similar congregations, though neither their participation nor approval is necessary. Deacons (or, sometimes, elders) are generally assigned the responsibility of watching over the spiritual and material needs of the local congregation. Their office is usually regarded as purely local. Congregationalists, as most other Protestants, deny that ordination imparts special grace to a man.

Two basic ideas are behind the congregational view of the ministry. One is that Christ is the Head of His church and, as such, is in living and vital contact with it. As our physical heads need no intermediary to control our bodies, so it is with the Head of the church and *His* body. It is not two or three officials, but two or three *believers,* gathered together in His name, in whose midst Christ promises to be (Matt. 18:20).

The second basic idea, common to most other Protestants as well, is the priesthood of all believers. Strictly speaking, there are no laymen in the church. All believers are priests (1 Peter 2:9)—that is, representatives of God to witness and minister to men in His name and power.

Further, the emphasis in the New Testament seems to be on the local church. There is no evidence of presbyterial or episcopal control of the church as a whole. Bishops and elders appear to have exercised their control within a local congregation, but not beyond it. The episcopal system did not appear until the second century.

Almost all churches fit into one of the above three groupings so far as polity is concerned.

Church Ordinances

There are numerous differences of opinion about the number and nature of "ordinances" in the church. Ordinances—some call them "sacraments"—are outward rites that signify or represent spiritual grace or blessing. The Roman Catholic church has seven sacraments: baptism, the Lord's Supper, confirmation, penance, orders, matrimony, and extreme unction. Protestants maintain, however, that Scripture recognizes only two ordinances—baptism and the Lord's Supper.

Roman Catholics teach that objective merit or grace is conferred by the sacraments. In contrast to this mechanical, almost magical, view, most Protestants emphasize faith and the working of God directly in the believer.

The meaning of baptism is perhaps most fully explained in Romans 6:1-4 (though some Christians insist that this chapter does not have baptism with water in view). Baptism has been called "an outward sign of an inward grace," a declaration and public identification with Christ in His death, burial, and resurrection. Protestants are divided on the issue of baptism: should it be only for those who make a profession of faith in Christ, or shouldn't infants be baptized? Episcopalians, Presbyterians, Lutherans, Methodists, and certain others practice infant baptism, whereas Baptists, Disciples, and a great number of independent churches hold to baptism of believers only. However, those who are baptized as infants often later make some public declaration of faith, usually as they enter into church membership.

Most Christians agree on their obligation to observe the Lord's request, "Do this in remembrance of Me." The Lord's Supper was to be a memorial and a "showing forth," or declaration, of His death till He returns (1 Cor. 11:23-26).

Roman Catholics teach that in the Lord's Supper the bread and wine become the *actual* body and blood of our Lord, though their appearance remains the same. This view is called *transubstantiation.* They further teach that the body and blood of Christ are offered every time a mass is observed. Scripture, however, emphatically contradicts such ideas. Christ's death on the cross was a complete and fully effective sacrifice, and He died once for all (Heb. 10:10; cf. 7:27; 9:12).

Lutherans believe in *consubstantiation.* In this view, Christ is present *with* the unchanged substance of the bread.

Most Protestants, however, believe either that the elements are only a symbolic memorial or that by faith the believer, in the Communion, enters into a special spiritual union with the glorified Christ.

Though participation in neither of these ordinances is necessary for salvation, every true believer should want to show his devotion to Christ by giving public witness in baptism and by remembering Him in the Lord's Supper.

Each genuine Christian, regardless of denomination, is spiritually one with every other believer. All are in the church universal. We are united in Christ, who is our life. There is no such thing as "lone-wolf" Christianity. If we are obedient to our Lord, we will identify with and join other believers for worship and service. In so doing, we not only contribute our own unique gifts to the fellowship to be used by God to help bless others, but are ourselves blessed.

CHAPTER EIGHT

Angels, Satan, and Demons

any Christians and others use "guardian angel" as a common expression, often quite seriously and sincerely, yet without much understanding of an angel's true existence. A group of people in San Francisco perversely established a Church of Satan complete with a minister who calls himself a high priest of Satan. We also know that among primitive peoples demons and evil spirits are worshiped, prayed to, and feared.

Are angels, the devil, and demons the result of ignorant superstition, or are they objective realities? The Bible speaks clearly about each of these types of spiritual beings. They can affect a Christian, and he is well advised to understand clearly who and what they are. Otherwise he may be in danger of being victimized by popular ideas that are totally erroneous and harmful.

Angels

Angels are mentioned in both the Old and the New Testaments. Jesus Himself referred to them many times. Speaking about "little ones," Jesus said, "Their angels in heaven always see the face of My Father" (Matt. 18:10). Concerning His return to earth in the last days, He said, "No one knows about

101

that day or hour, not even the angels in heaven" (Mark 13:32). Other references He made to angels are recorded in Mark 8:38; Matthew 13:41; 26:53.

Angels are created beings: "For by Him all things were created: things in heaven and on earth, visible and invisible, whether thrones or powers or rulers or authorities; all things were created by Him and for Him" (Col. 1:16). Angels probably preceded man in creation; Satan, presumably a fallen angel, visited the Garden of Eden to tempt man. The words "In the beginning God created the heavens and the earth" probably include the creation of angels, though they are not specifically mentioned.

Unlike man, who is composed of body and spirit, angels are incorporeal (purely spirit) beings: "Are not all angels ministering spirits sent to serve those who will inherit salvation?" (Heb. 1:14) They at times take bodily form, as when two angels came to Lot in Sodom (Gen. 19:1), and sometimes they become visible, as at the Resurrection (John 20:12). Such appearances, however, were exceptions rather than the rule.

Though the masculine gender is always used with the word *angel*, there is no distinction of sex with these beings. Jesus implied this when He said of resurrected believers, "At the resurrection people will neither marry nor be given in marriage; they will be like the angels in heaven" (Matt. 22:30).

Angels are eternal; they never die. They are not subject to aging, and in heaven we shall be like them in this respect: "Neither can [the saved in heaven] die anymore; for they are equal unto the angels" (Luke 20:36, KJV).

In God's order of creation, angels are higher than man. God has made man a little lower than the angels (Ps. 8:5). But redeemed man, as part of the new creation, is higher than the angels and will have authority over them: "Do you not know that we will judge angels?" (1 Cor. 6:3)

The intelligence and power of angels are greater than man's, though they are limited or finite. This truth is implied in our Lord's statement that the angels, though they are in heaven, do not know the day or the hour of the end time (Mark 13:32). The Gospel and salvation are things the angels "desire to look into" (1 Peter 1:12, KJV). Angels are also referred to as greater in power and might than men (2 Peter 2:11). They excel in strength (Ps. 103:20). One angel killed 185,000 Assyrians in one night (Isa. 37:36). The angels' power is not theirs inherently, but comes by delegation from God. The Greek term translated "angel" means, literally, "messenger." Angels are basically messengers or servants of God. They are messengers of His might (cf. 2 Thes. 1:7).

Angels stand in the very presence of God. As mentioned, Jesus said they "always see the face of My Father" (Matt. 18:10). They are higher than men in this respect, and they continually worship God (cf. Rev. 5:11-12; Isa. 6:3). They also take pleasure in His works and grace, and show awareness of and interest in individual human beings. "There is rejoicing in the presence of the angels of God over one sinner who repents" (Luke 15:10).

Angelic Activity

The activity of angels on earth has a number of facets, though essentially it is concerned with the doing of God's will: "You His angels . . . who obey His word . . . you His servants who do His will" (Ps. 103:20-21).

Angels punish the enemies of God and execute His judgment, as Herod discovered when "the angel of the Lord smote him, because he gave not God the glory" (Acts 12:23). God sent an angel to destroy Jerusalem in David's time (1 Chron. 21:15).

A more comforting truth is the relationship of angels to individual believers. Angels protected Daniel because of his faithfulness to God. To the amazed Darius, who appeared at the lion pit expecting to find him dead, Daniel said, "My God sent His angel, and shut the lions' mouths. They have not hurt me" (Dan. 6:22). An angel provided for distraught and hungry Elijah: "An angel touched him and said, 'Get up and eat' " (1 Kings 19:5). Peter was twice released from prison by an angel (Acts 5:19; 12:8-11). From these instances and others, we see how angels defend, protect, and deliver God's servants when it is in His providence to do so.

Angels may guide Christians to witness to a certain unbeliever, as an angel led Philip to the Ethiopian (Acts 8:26). Angels may also guide an unbeliever to a Christian, as when Cornelius and Peter were brought together.

In the midst of a shipboard crisis, Paul was cheered by an angel in the night (Acts 27:23). During His agony in the garden, our Lord Himself was strengthened by an angel (Luke 22:43).

Angels are also concerned with the church and its activity. Paul charged Timothy, concerning his ministry: "I charge you, in the sight of God and Christ Jesus and the elect angels, to keep these instructions" (1 Tim. 5:21).

Angels will accompany Christ when He comes in glory and in judgment. "When the Son of man comes . . . and all the angels with Him, He will sit on His throne" (Matt. 25:31).

No number of the angels is given in Scripture, but it is clear that they are many. Daniel, of his vision of God, said, "Thousands upon thousands attended Him; ten thousand times ten thousand stood before Him" (Dan. 7:10). John reported of *his* vision, "I looked and heard the voice of many angels, numbering thousands upon thousands, and ten thousand times ten thousand" (Rev. 5:11).

Among this vast number of angels there is organization and rank. Jesus said that had He so desired He could summon more than twelve legions of angels (Matt. 26:53). References to the hosts of heaven in the Old Testament imply organization. Micaiah said, "I saw the Lord sitting on His throne with all the host of heaven standing around Him on His right hand and on His left" (1 Kings 22:19).

The statement about "thrones or powers or rulers or authorities" (Col. 1:16) seems to indicate ranking. These orders of heavenly beings are viewed as good, being God-ordained. Evil beings seem to have similar organization and ranking: "Our struggle is not against flesh and blood, but against the rulers, against the authorities, against the powers of this dark world and against the spiritual forces of evil in the heavenly realms" (Eph. 6:12).

Other Angelic Beings

Michael is the only archangel mentioned in Scripture. He is considered as a special guardian of Israel and as "one of the chief princes" (Dan. 10:13, 21). He contended with the devil for the body of Moses (Jude 9). It may have been Michael who spoke to Moses on Mount Sinai, or Horeb (Ex. 3:2). He led the battle in heaven against Satan (Rev. 12:7).

Apocryphal, Babylonian, and Persian sources mention seven archangels. That only one archangel is mentioned in the Bible indicates that the biblical doctrine of angels was not derived from secular sources, as some critics suggest.

The only other angel named in the Bible is Gabriel, renowned for blowing his horn. Presumably this association comes from 1 Thessalonians 4:16, where Christ's return is said to be accompanied by "the voice of the archangel and with the trumpet call of God." Gabriel appears in the Old Testament as the one commissioned to explain the vision of the ram and the he-goat to Daniel (Dan. 8:16) and to declare the prophecy of the seventy weeks (9:21-27). In the New Testament he announced two great births—of John to Zachariah and Elizabeth and of Jesus to Mary (Luke 1:19, 26-33). Gabriel evidently has high rank as one who continually stands in the very presence of the Lord (Luke 1:19). His function seems to be that of a messenger, while Michael's appears to be that of a warrior.

Angels are never mediators between man and God, and men are not to worship them. Certain ancient Greek philosophers developed a whole series of graded emanations or spirits through which men could make contact with God. These philosophers maintained that God is much too holy to have anything to do with material things in general, and with earth and man in particular. Ancient Zoroastrianism taught a similar belief. This sort of doctrine is totally foreign to the Bible's teaching, however. Angels are God's messengers, but this in no way implies that He has no direct contact with men when He so chooses. We need approach God through no other medium but Jesus Christ.

In most popular thinking and art, angels are winged creatures. There is little biblical warrant for this notion. In Scripture, angels most often appear in manlike form. The only winged beings mentioned in Scripture are *cherubim* and *seraphim* (the singular forms are *cherub* and *seraph*). We do not have a great deal of information about either. God stationed cherubim at the east entrance of the Garden of Eden with a flaming sword to guard the tree of life (Gen. 3:24). In Ezekiel's vision (chaps. 1; 10), cherubim are called "living creatures." Each cherub is described as having four faces—of man, lion, ox, and eagle. Each has four wings; two are stretched upward and two downward to cover his body.

Seraphim are mentioned in Isaiah's vision of the heavenly temple. They have six wings and can fly (Isa. 6:2, 6). These beings apparently were human in form, apart from their wings, and were associated with the cherubim in guarding the divine throne. It is possible that the cherubim and seraphim are in some way related to the living creatures in heaven (Rev. 4–5).

Contrary to a popular mythology, there is absolutely no scriptural warrant for the idea that a person becomes an angel after he dies.

The question often arises as to whether angels appear today as they did in biblical times. Experience does not indicate that such appearances are usual. There is, however, no biblical teaching that rules out this possibility. It would be wise, however, to maintain an attitude of healthy skepticism toward any story of an angelic appearance, unless the report were independently verified. Sometimes impressionable people have hallucinations, and sometimes they embellish their stories unwittingly in retelling them.

"One story about angels which seems to be authentic has to do with the well-known missionary to the New Hebrides, John G. Paton. Since he had aroused the enmity of the local native chief by his successes in the Gospel, the chief hired a man to kill the missionary. The man went to the missionary's house, but instead of murdering Paton he returned in terror, saying he had seen a row of men, dressed in white, surrounding the missionary's home. The chief thought the man had drunk too much whiskey and encouraged him to try again. The next time others of the tribe accompanied him. That night they all saw three rows of men surrounding Paton's home.

"When the chief asked the missionary where he kept the men in the daytime who surrounded his house at night, Paton, knowing nothing of what had happened, disclaimed the whole idea. When the chief, in amazement, told his story, the missionary realized the natives had seen an angelic company which God had sent to protect him, and he related it to Psalm 34:7: 'The angel of the Lord encamps around those who fear Him [God], and he delivers them.' The savages were powerfully impressed with the missionary's explanation, as well they might be."[1]

Evil Spiritual Beings

God created angels perfect, and they were originally uncorrupted in spirit. At the same time, they had free will and were susceptible to temptation and sin. How sin could have come into the experience of a perfect creature is a mystery, but that it actually happened is clear.

Peter warns against apostasy on the basis of God's judgment on angels (2 Peter 2:4), and we read of angels who "did not keep their positions of authority but abandoned their own home" (Jude 6). Some feel that this angelic fall took place after Creation (Gen. 1:1) and that because of it the original Creation became "formless and empty" (v. 2). The cause of the angels' fall is not specified, but presumably is related to the fall of Satan.

The name *Satan* means "adversary" or "opponent." Peter calls him "your enemy the devil" (1 Peter 5:8). Joshua stood before the angel of the Lord, with "Satan standing at his right side to accuse him" (Zech. 3:1). Satan is the opposer and enemy of both God and His people.

It has been fashionable, in recent years, to consider belief in the existence and personality of Satan as primitive, naive, and even superstitious. It is suggested instead that Satan, if we must use the term, is only the personification of the evil in the world. This notion has resulted partly from reaction to extravagant ideas and poetic expressions about Satan that were prominent during the Middle Ages. But these distorted ideas have no basis in Scripture, our only source of authoritative information.

Nowhere does the Bible depict Satan as a red man with horns, a tail, and a pitchfork. Some suggest that these caricatures are part of Satan's wiles to persuade sophisticated twentieth-century men that he doesn't exist. People's incredulity makes his job that much less difficult.

Biblically, there can be no doubt as to the devil's existence and personality. He is presented as appearing before the Lord when God challenged him about Job (Job 1:6-12; 2:1-7). There is no mistaking Satan's reality in his temptation of our Lord in the wilderness. He spoke to Jesus and Jesus spoke to him (Matt. 4:1-11).

Satan's Other Names

Satan's other scriptural names also indicate his reality and personality. The only other proper name given him is *Devil*. Other terms applied to him describe him and his work. He is *the tempter* (1 Thes. 3:5). He is the *wicked one* who snatches away the good seed of the Word of God out of people's hearts (Matt. 13:19). He is the *enemy* who sows tares among the good seed (Matt. 13:39). He is our *adversary* (1 Peter 5:8). Jesus calls him the *father of lies* and a *murderer* (John 8:44). He is the *supreme deceiver* (Rev. 12:9).

Belial (2 Cor. 6:15) and *Beelzebub* (Matt. 12:24) have obscure derivations, but are used as synonyms for Satan. They denote a wicked person.

Demon Possession

In modern times, many theologians regard demon possession as only a primitive, prescientific description of what we now call mental illness. Throughout history, undoubtedly, some victims of mental illness have been wrongly accused of demon possession, and so treated harshly. But we should guard against confusion of the two conditions.

Some people suggest that all sickness is initiated and caused by demons, but the New Testament makes clear distinctions: "People brought to Him all who were ill with various diseases, those suffering severe pain, the demon-possessed, those having seizures, the paralyzed, and He healed them" (Matt. 4:24). Here clear differentiation is made between ordinary diseases and demon possession, and between demon possession and lunacy.

On another occasion Jesus cast out a demon who had caused dumbness (Matt. 9:32-33). From this account it is clear that the results of demon possession are not exclusively mental or nervous. Nor does the Bible connect epilepsy and demon possession. The boy Jesus healed of fits (Matt. 17:15-18) seems to have been afflicted with more than epilepsy. The Gadarene maniac (Mark 5:1-20), and possibly the man who overpowered two sons of the exorcist, Sceva (Acts 19:16), in addition to being demon-possessed, may also have been mentally ill.

Demon possession is seldom mentioned in the Old Testament, the Book of Acts, or the Epistles. The incidents of it centered around our Lord's ministry and may indicate a special attack on mankind by Satan during that period.

Demon possession is a worldwide phenomenon, however, with authenticated contemporary cases being reported in the United States as well as in other parts of the world. It is indeed possible deliberately to open oneself to demons. Trifling with the occult or playing around the edges of the spirit world are dangerous practices, and Christians should carefully avoid them.

We should never try to conquer demons by our own power. Even the disciples had some frustrating encounters with such spirits. Jesus said, "This kind can come forth by nothing, but by prayer and fasting" (Mark 9:29, KJV). Generally, evil spirits were exorcised by being commanded to come out in the name of Christ (e.g., Acts 16:18). It has been suggested that rather than attempt to exorcise a satanic spirit ourselves, even in the name of Christ, we should ask God to do so for us. Even Michael the archangel did this (Jude 9).

A demon-possessed person invariably acts in ways that are not natural and normal to him. He often speaks in a voice entirely different from his normal one, and sometimes displays superhuman strength. He may also have powers of telepathy and clairvoyance. It should be noted that possession, in every instance, is by demons or evil spirits, never by good spirits.

Despite the great power of Satan and his demons, however, a Christian need not fear them if he is in close fellowship with the Lord. The Holy Spirit's presence in us is a reality and insures our safety (1 John 4:4).

These truths are clear from scriptural teachings and their implications about Satan and demons:

First, Satan's power over a believer is limited. The devil could not touch Job without God's permission (Job 1:9-12; 2:4-6). Demons had to ask permission of Christ to enter swine (Mark 5:12). Satan is not all-powerful.

Neither is the devil all-knowing. If he were, he would have known in advance the futility of his scheme to subvert Job, and he would surely have realized that it was useless for him to tempt the Lord in the wilderness.

Satan was conquered by Christ: John wrote, "The reason the Son of God appeared was to destroy the devil's work" (1 John 3:8).

Satan is slated for final eternal judgment: "And the devil, who deceived them, was thrown into the lake of burning sulfur, where the beast and the false prophet had been thrown. They will be tormented day and night for ever and ever" (Rev. 20:10).

Because Satan has been overcome by Christ, Christians are encouraged by God's promise that if they resist the devil he will flee (James 4:7). But our resistance must be "standing firm in the faith" (1 Peter 5:9). We can best thwart Satan's designs on us by daily yielding ourselves to the Lord in prayer and by putting on the whole armor of God (Eph. 6:10-17).

We should avoid the extreme of trying to see Satan behind every misfortune, in this way evading our personal responsibility. Equally dangerous, however, is being so lulled by the sophistication of our age that we are unaware of Satan and his wiles against us in the spiritual battle in which every true believer is engaged.

CHAPTER NINE

Salvation

rom one point of view, salvation is very simple. It can be summed up in Paul's words to the Philippian jailer: "Believe in the Lord Jesus, and you will be saved" (Acts 16:31). At the same time, salvation is profound; it has the most pervasive and permanent impact possible on the one who experiences it. We do not, of course, have to understand all the aspects of salvation before we can receive it. We may understand very little when we first trust Christ. And there are some things we will not understand until we see our Lord face to face. But studying God's Word and trying to understand more fully the truth of our salvation greatly enriches us spiritually.

Several theological terms are generally used in connection with salvation. Each contributes something and, taken together, they give a greater fullness of God's light. None of these terms or truths can be isolated completely from the others. We should always study them in context. We cannot always be dogmatic about the order or sequence in which an individual should experience these various aspects of salvation, for they often overlap and sometimes are simply different views of the same truth.

Repentance

John the Baptist began his ministry with a call to *repentance:* "Repent, for the kingdom of heaven is near" (Matt. 3:2). Jesus began preaching with the identical words (Matt. 4:17). He commanded His disciples that "repentance and forgiveness of sins should be preached in His name to all nations, beginning at Jerusalem" (Luke 24:47). Peter took up this message on the Day of Pentecost (Acts 2:38). Paul points out that now God "commands all people everywhere to repent" (Acts 17:30; cf. 26:20). Acceptance of the Gospel, means "both Jews and Greeks . . . must turn to God in repentance and have faith in our Lord Jesus" (Acts 20:21).

The word used in the Old Testament for *repentance* means "to turn or return." It implies a personal decision to turn away from sin and *to* God. In the New Testament, the terms *repent* and *repentance* that apply to man's relationship to sin and God have the basic meaning of a change of mind. They imply a change of mind about sin, and a turning to God. In a sense, they are the negative and positive aspects of the same truth. The two together are inseparable and complementary. Paul, in his defense before Agrippa, said he preached that both Jews and Gentiles "should repent and turn to God and prove their repentance by their deeds" (Acts 26:20).

True repentance is not merely a feeling of remorse, such as Judas had after he betrayed the Lord. It involves the intellect, the emotions, and the will.

Repentance brings the mind to realize both the holiness of God's Law and one's utter failure and inability to keep it. It may also involve a change of mind as to who Christ is, as was true with the Jews on the Day of Pentecost (Acts 2:14-40). They had formerly viewed Jesus as an impostor, but Peter called on them to accept Him as Messiah and Saviour.

The emotions are involved in repentance. "Godly sorrow," in contrast to one's being superficially sorry for sin, often precedes the change of mind: "Godly sorrow brings repentance that leaves no regret" The *Good News Bible* terms it "sadness that is used by God" bring "a change of heart" (2 Cor. 7:10). Repentance involves a feeling of the awfulness of sin in its effect on man and his relationship to God. Emotion, however, is no gauge of the extent of one's repentance. The presence or absence of tears does not necessarily indicate genuineness or lack of it. But when we truly repent we are sure to experience some feeling about it.

Repentance involves the will. The prodigal son not only came to his senses intellectually and regretted what he had done, but he *acted*: "I will arise and go to my father. . . . And he arose" (Luke 15:18, 20, KJV). Repentance is deliberate, willful turning away from sin and following after God. True repentance always leads to a change in conduct or attitude.

Faith

Repentance, if it is genuine, will lead to *faith*. In fact, some Christians understand "faith" to *include* repentance, pointing out that for a person to receive Christ as his Saviour in faith is in itself evidence that he is aware of his need, as a sinner, for the Saviour. The term *faith*, in its noun, verb, and adjective forms, is used dozens of times in the Old Testament, but occurs several hundred times in the New Testament. Its most common meaning is "confident trust in or reliance on."

Faith is central to the whole Christian experience: "Without faith it is impossible to please God, because anyone who comes to Him must believe that He exists and that He rewards those who earnestly seek Him" (Heb. 11:6). Faith, in the New Testament, always has as its background the person and work of Christ. He is the object of our faith, reliance, or trust. Whoever believes in Him will not perish, but has everlasting life (John 3:16). In and of itself, faith is meaningless. It always has an object to which it is directed and upon which it rests. If the object of our faith is worthless, we are victims of superstition, no matter how sincerely we believe.

Saving faith consists of several elements. First are the *facts* about Christ—His deity, His death, and our need of Him. We must accept these facts as *true*, though mere mental assent to this truth does not save us. James makes this clear: "You believe that there is one God. Good! Even the demons believe that—and shudder" (James 2:19). One could not possibly be a Christian without believing these basic facts, but saving faith goes beyond mere belief *about* Christ to complete commitment *to* and trust *in* Him. Such commitment involves the *will* as well as the mind and the emotions. One does not believe simply because of one's feelings—one *decides* to believe.

Faith is the instrument that links us to Christ. The New Testament emphasizes that we are saved by *faith* and not by *works*. "However, to the man who does not work but trusts God who justifies the wicked, his faith is credited as righteousness" (Rom. 4:5).

At first sight, the Epistle of James appears to disagree: "What good is it, my brothers, if a man claims to have faith but has no deeds? Can such faith save him? . . . You see that a person is justified by what he does and not by faith alone" (James 2:14, 24).

The "faith" James criticizes is "head belief "—mere intellectual assent to facts. Such "faith" does not lead to holy living and hence is "dead" or "useless" (James 2:20). It has no saving value. When we read about "faith" in the other epistles, wholehearted trust in Christ is in view. This is the faith on the basis of which God credits a believer with righteousness, leading its possessor to want a holy life.

When we read that we are saved by faith rather than by "works," the works in view are the keeping of the Law in an effort to earn salvation. James (2:14, 18, 20) does not use the term *works* in this sense. His "works" are very much like "the fruit of the Spirit" of which Paul speaks (Gal. 5:22). Leon Morris points out: "They are warm deeds of love springing from a right attitude to God. They are the fruits of faith. What James objects to is the claim that faith is there when there is no fruit to attest it."[1]

How does faith come about? "Faith comes from hearing the message, and the message is heard through the word of Christ" (Rom. 10:17). In the days of the apostles, "many who heard the message believed" (Acts 4:4). God uses His Word, both spoken and written, to produce faith. At the same time, "God hath dealt to every man the measure of faith" (Rom. 12:3,

KJV), which implies that faith is a work of God.

In almost every phase of salvation there is a mysterious interplay between the divine and human sides. It is not always possible, though, to draw neat lines of distinction. For instance, we may think of *repentance* and *faith* as man's response to *regeneration*, which God produces.

Regeneration

"Regeneration, or the new birth, is the divine side of that change of heart which, viewed from the human side, we call conversion," according to Strong.[2] The term is used only twice in the New Testament—of the restoration of the world (Matt. 19:28) and of the renewal or rebirth of individuals: "He saved us, not because of righteous things we had done, but because of His mercy. He saved us through the washing of rebirth and renewal by the Holy Spirit" (Titus 3:5).

Sin is so serious that a sinner cannot even see the kingdom of God, let alone enter it, unless he is born from above, or born again (John 3:3)—as Jesus pointed out in His conversation with the Jewish leader, Nicodemus. God takes the initiative in regeneration, or rebirth, but man must actively respond in faith. "But as many as received Him, to them gave He power to become the sons of God, even to them that believe on His name, which were born, not of blood, nor of the will of the flesh, nor of the will of man, but of God" (John 1:12-13, KJV). "God, who is rich in mercy, made us alive with Christ even when we were dead in trangressions" (Eph. 2:4-5).

The new birth results not in a change of personality as such, but in a whole new way of life. Before the new birth, self and sin are in control; but after it, the Holy Spirit is in control. A born-again person shares in the very life of God. He becomes a "partaker of the divine nature" (2 Peter 1:4, KJV), and is described as a "new creation" (2 Cor. 5:17); he puts on "the new self, created to be like God in true righteousness and holiness" (Eph. 4:24; cf. Col. 3:10). Regeneration is a decisive experience that happens once for all, though it has continuing results in the life of a Christian.

God "wants all men to be saved and to come to a knowledge of the truth" (1 Tim. 2:4). That some men are not regenerated or reborn is not God's fault. The responsibility rests with men. Our Lord diagnosed this problem. When speaking to a typical group, He said, "These Scriptures . . . testify about Me, yet you *refuse* to come to Me to have life" (John 5:40, italics added). It wasn't that they *could* not have come, but that they *would* not. They deliberately refused to believe the message delivered to them.

How men actually come to faith in Christ is a profound question. Some, by approaching the problem entirely from man's side, have tended to eclipse the sovereignty of God. Others, by approaching it only from God's side, have seemed to obliterate man's freedom.

We need to understand several theological terms to avoid confusion and popular misconceptions. These terms are *election, predestination,* and *foreknowledge.*

Election

Election has to do with God's choice of certain groups and people to receive His grace. This choice is based on His sovereign pleasure and not on the value, goodness, or disposition of those chosen. In the Old Testament, God's election is illustrated in His choice of Abraham, with whom He made an everlasting covenant, and of Abraham's descendants, the nation of Israel, to have a special relationship with Himself (Gen. 11:31–12:7).

Election, as used in the New Testament, has to do with God's choice of particular individuals for salvation. Jesus said, "And He will send His angels and gather His elect from the four winds" (Mark 13:27). Christians are "chosen [elect] according to the foreknowledge of God the Father" (1 Peter 1:2). God "chose [elected] us in Him before the creation of the world. . . . In love He predestined us to be adopted as His sons through Jesus Christ, in accordance with His pleasure and will" (Eph. 1:4-5). Jesus Himself explicitly said, "You did not choose Me, but I chose you" (John 15:16).

Predestination and Foreknowledge

Closely allied to election are *predestination* and *foreknowledge*. Predestination is a term used only of Christians. It indicates that God's purpose for a believer—that he become Christlike—is sure to be fulfilled. "For those God foreknew He also predestined to be conformed to the likeness of His Son. . . . And . . . those He called, He also justified; those He justified, He also glorified" (Rom. 8:29-30). Foreknowledge, predestination, calling, justification, and glorification are all grouped together in one "package." A person who has *one* of them has them *all*. The sequence indicates that apart from the grace of God we cannot trust in Christ. Jesus said, "No one can come to Me unless the Father who sent Me draws him" (John 6:44).

Like election, *predestination* is according to God's sovereign purpose and will. It is not based on any merits in those persons whom He has chosen.

It is important to realize that *all* men are sinners and are under the judgment of God. "God in sovereign freedom treats some sinners as they deserve . . . but He selects others to be "objects of His mercy," receiving the "riches of His glory" (Rom. 9:23). This discrimination involves no injustice, for the Creator owes mercy to none and has a right to do as He pleases with His rebellious creatures (Rom. 9:14-21). The wonder is not that He withholds mercy from some, but that He should be gracious to any."[3]

The purpose of the Bible's teaching on election and predestination is to lead pardoned sinners to worship God for the grace they have experienced. They come to see, in unmistakable terms, that salvation is *all* of God and not at all of themselves. They also come to see that since they were chosen in Christ before the foundation of the world, their election is eternal and therefore certain. This inspires devotion and love to Christ in gratitude for God's unfathomable love.

The popular misconception of election and predestination as the arbitrary acts of a capricious tyrant is totally foreign and unfair to Scripture. The attitude often expressed by unbelievers is that if they are elect, they'll get into heaven anyway, and if they're not, there's no use in their trying. In either case, they reason, they needn't be concerned. This is a tragic misconception. No one in hell will be able to tell God, "I wanted to be saved, but my name was on the wrong list."

Election and predestination are always to salvation and its blessings—never to judgment. It is true that no one believes on the Saviour unless God the Holy Spirit convicts him, but it is also true that those who do not trust Christ choose not to believe. God never refuses to save anyone who wants salvation.

Some feel that the expression, "chosen according to the foreknowledge of God" (1 Peter 1:2), means that God elects to salvation those whom He knows in advance will respond positively to the Gospel. But foreknowledge is not the same thing as foreordination or election.

Throughout church history, honest differences of opinion have arisen about these complex and not-fully-explainable doctrines. Each believer should be persuaded in his own mind about them, and should show a charitable spirit toward those who differ with him.

A conversation between Charles Simeon and John Wesley, on December 20, 1784 is helpful at this point:

Simeon said: "Sir, I understand that you are called an Arminian; and I have sometimes been called a Calvinist; and therefore I suppose we are to draw daggers. But before I consent to begin the combat, with your permission, I will ask you a few questions. . . . Pray, Sir, do you feel yourself a depraved creature, so depraved that you would never have thought of turning to God if God had not first put it in your heart?"

"Yes," said Wesley, "I do indeed."

"And do you utterly despair of recommending yourself to God by anything you can do, and look for salvation solely through the blood and righteousness of Christ?"

"Yes, solely through Christ."

"But, Sir, supposing you were at first saved by Christ, are you not somehow or other to save yourself afterwards by your own works?"

"No, I must be saved by Christ from first to last."

"Allowing, then, that you were first turned by the grace of God, are you not in some way or other to keep yourself by your own power?"

"No."

"What then? Are you to be upheld every hour and every moment by God, as much as an infant in its mother's arms?"

"Yes, altogether."

"And is all your hope in the grace and mercy of God to preserve you unto His heavenly kingdom?"

"Yes, I have no hope but in Him."

"Then, Sir, with your leave I will put up my dagger again; for this is all my Calvinism; this is my election, my justification by faith, my final perseverance: it is in substance all that I hold, and as I hold it; and therefore, if you please, instead of searching out terms and phrases to be a ground of contention between us, we will cordially unite in those things wherein we agree."[4]

The experience of salvation, in relation to the divine and human factors, includes some ambiguities. The results of salvation, however, are very clear. There are three phases of salvation: past, present, and future. That we have *been* saved, that we are *being* saved, and that we *shall be* saved are all true statements. Each refers to a particular aspect of salvation.

Justification

Justification has often been defined as meaning, "Just as if I'd never sinned." This aspect involves acquittal, but justification goes even further by declaring a person to be *righteous*. When God justifies us, He does not merely forgive our sins, making us neutral—moral and spiritual zeroes. He sees us in Christ as having His perfect righteousness. Justification has to do with our standing before God, and is *objective*. It does not make one *personally* righteous, but it *declares* him righteous in a legal sense, and brings him into right relationship with God.

Paul, to whom justification is central in salvation, stresses that we cannot be justified by the works of the Law, for "no one will be declared righteous in [God's] sight by observing the Law; rather, through the Law we become conscious of sin" (Rom. 3:20). Rather, we are "justified freely by [God's] grace through the redemption that came by Christ Jesus" (Rom. 3:24).

The *basis*, or ground, of our justification, or being declared righteous, is twofold. Christ's death as our substitute satisfied the claims of God's holy Law against our sin. "While we were still sinners, Christ died for us. Since we have now been justified by His blood, how much more shall we be saved from God's wrath through Him!" (Rom. 5:8-9)

The other basis of God's declaring us righteous is Christ's perfect obedience: "Just as through the disobedience of the one man [Adam] the many [i.e., all men] were made sinners, so also through the obedience of the one man [Christ] the many [i.e., all who believe] will be made righteous" (Rom. 5:19). Christ became identified with us when He was made sin for us on the cross; and we are identified with Him in His newness of resurrection life, and share His righteousness.

We are justified by faith. This truth burst upon the heart and mind of Martin Luther like a bombshell as he considered the words: "Therefore, since we have been justified through faith, we have peace with God through our Lord Jesus Christ" (Rom. 5:1). After long struggling in unsuccessful self-effort to win the favor of God, Luther suddenly realized it was not what *he* could do, but what *God* had done, that made justification and peace possible. The Protestant Reformation resulted from this discovery.

The fact that we have been justified becomes clear through the evidence of our changed lives, marked by obedience to God and desire to do His will. When we say that we have been saved, we are referring to our justification. Paul wrote to the Ephesians, "For it is by grace you have been saved, through faith" (Eph. 2:8). Paul's certainty of a past event, based on what God had done, led him to overflow with assurance. He wrote, "For I am convinced that neither death nor life, neither angels nor demons, neither the present nor the future, nor any powers, neither height nor depth, nor anything else in all creation, will be able to separate us from the love of God that is in Christ Jesus our Lord" (Rom. 8:38-39). We too may enjoy such assurance, for our salvation is an accomplished fact if we are in Christ.

Sanctification

But we are also *being* saved. This process of becoming holy is called *sanctification.* Justification has to do with our standing before God and is instantaneous. Sanctification has to do with our character and conduct and is progressive. It continues as long as we live.

Basically, the word *sanctified* means "set apart." The term *saint* comes from the same root and means "a set-apart one." Another word with the same meaning is *holy.*

"Sanctify" is used in two ways:

1. To set apart, or declare holy, for God's use or service. Christians are called "saints" in this sense—God has set them apart for His service. Such "sanctification" is usually regarded as being instantaneous and as taking place at the time of one's conversion: "You were washed, you were sanctified, you were justified in the name of the Lord Jesus and by the Spirit of our God" (1 Cor. 6:11).

2. To make the personal life of an individual Christian holy, in the sense of moral and spiritual improvement. This is a lifelong process. We are to "grow in the grace, and knowledge of our Lord and Saviour Jesus Christ" (2 Peter 3:18), and as we mature spiritually we are "transformed into [Christ's] likeness with ever-increasing glory, which comes from the Lord, who is the Spirit" (2 Cor. 3:18).

Some feel that sanctification is a crisis experience, as is justification, and that one can experience "entire sanctification" in a moment of time. Differences of opinion on this question hinge almost completely on the definition of sin and on the standard of holy living meant. *Sin* is often defined as "any voluntary transgression of a known law," as Wesley put it. The Westminster Shorter Catechism, on the other hand, defines *sin* as "any want of conformity unto or transgression of the Law of God." This definition includes sins of omission and also takes our sinful nature into consideration—as well as overt sins committed deliberately.

Another big question has to do with *how* God sanctifies us. Those who say the process is all of God tend to minimize human responsibility. On the other hand, those who tend to minimize sin exaggerate human responsibility in sanctification.

A key principle that recognizes both God's initiative and man's responsibility is expressed in the scriptural command, "Continue to work out your salvation with fear and trembling, for it is God who works in you to will and to act according to His good purpose" (Phil. 2:12-13). It is because God works in him that man is able to work. On the other hand, although God enables, man must respond. He is to show neither supine passivity nor naive confidence in his own effort.

Justification, declaring us righteous, delivers us from the *penalty* of sin. Sanctification, involving the development of holiness of character, delivers us from the *power* of sin. But how does holiness become *real* in our daily experience? Paul portrays the personal struggle vividly (Rom. 7) and also gives the remedy for it. He says that Christ died "in order that the righteous requirements of the Law might be fully met in us, who do not live according to the sinful nature but according to the Spirit" (Rom. 8:4). God's command is, "Live by the Spirit, and you will not gratify the desires of the sinful nature" (Gal. 5:16). The Holy Spirit gives us power to overcome sin and produces in us the fruit of the Spirit (Gal. 5:22-23). This "walk" is a life of daily faith in which we claim and live personally what has already been given us by God. Christ has been made to us "wisdom, and righteousness, and sanctification, and redemption" (1 Cor. 1:30).

As we depend on Christ, then, His patience, love, power, purity, etc. will begin to show in our attitudes and conduct. He does not dole out these qualities to us in "little packages"—we have all of them we need in Christ, who indwells us. "His divine power has given unto us *everything* we need for life and *godliness* through our knowledge of Him who called us by His own glory and goodness" (2 Peter 1:3, italics added).

The key principle in sanctification, as in justification, is faith, i.e., confident trust and reliance on Jesus Christ. We can be *saved* only by faith and we can *live effectively* as Christians only by faith. "Just as you received Christ Jesus as Lord [by faith], continue to live in Him" (Col. 2:6). God, in both instances, does what we cannot do. Our part is to respond in faith.

Glorification

But there is a sense in which salvation is also future: we *shall* be saved. We have been saved from the *penalty* of sin; we are being saved from the *power* of sin; and we shall be saved from the very *presence* of sin. We shall personally be perfect and free from all sin. "Dear friends, now we are children of God, and what we will be has not yet been made known. But we know that when He appears, we shall be like Him, for we shall see Him as He is" (1 John 3:2). It is in this sense that we are appointed "to *receive* salvation" (1 Thes. 5:9, italics added), and it is this salvation which is ready to be revealed in the last days and to which Paul refers when he writes that, "our salvation is nearer now than when we first believed" (Rom. 13:11). This complete and final sanctification, this deliverance from the very presence of sin is called *glorification*.

Salvation is God's great gift to man. Though in experience its aspects may not be separated, an understanding of its details gives a Christian deeper appreciation, greater love, and happier praise for the God who has saved him.

CHAPTER TEN

Things to Come

ne of the most fascinating features of the Bible is that it tells what is ahead. Both Old and New Testaments contend that history is moving to a climax and that the sovereign God is in control. Helmut Thielicke, in his book *The Waiting Father* sums up this truth in a magnificent way: "When the drama of history is over, Jesus Christ will stand alone upon the stage. All the great figures of history—Pharaoh, Alexander the Great, Charlemagne, Churchill, Stalin, Johnson, Mao Tse-tung—will realize they have been bit actors in a drama produced by Another."[1]

Throughout the Old Testament, the prophets looked forward to "the Day of the Lord," the time when God would exercise final judgment on Israel and other nations for their wickedness. All judgments—whether by means of invasion, plague, or natural disaster—will come to full flower at the return of Christ.

The Old Testament contains two lines of messianic prophecy. One pictures the Messiah (Christ) as the Suffering Servant (e.g., Isa. 53). The other regards Him as a reigning King (e.g., Isa. 9:6). The first coming of Christ, as the Suffering Servant, answered the hope for God's coming to redeem His people. The second coming of Christ will bring consummation of that hope when He returns as reigning King.

In the meantime, though, Satan has been conquered by

Christ—at the Cross and in the Resurrection—so that "by His death He might destroy him who holds the power of death— that is, the devil" (Heb. 2:14). But Satan is, temporarily, still "the god of this age" (2 Cor. 4:4), and he is actively opposing Christ and His church.

The Antichrist

Satan's opposition will culminate in the appearance of a being called Antichrist. The "spirit of Antichrist" is to be abroad before this person appears. In fact, his presence was noted already in apostolic times: "Dear children, this is the last hour; and as you have heard that the Antichrist is coming, even now many antichrists have come. This is how we know it is the last hour" (1 John 2:18). Of this Antichrist it is asked, "Who is the liar? It is the man who denies that Jesus is the Christ. Such a man is the Antichrist—he denies the Father and the Son" (v. 22).

Though there is considerable difference of opinion among Bible scholars, some feel, because of the similarity of description given in Daniel 11:37 and 2 Thessalonians 2:4, that these passages refer to the same person. If these also refer to the same person as "the beast" (Rev. 13:3, 13, 16-17), several striking characteristics emerge. Satan, with a view to deceiving and persuading men, will inspire Antichrist and give him power to act supernaturally. As an ecclesiastical leader, he will manipulate religion for his own ends, so as to claim the worship due God. He will also demand political allegiance and will exercise economic pressure to force compliance (Rev. 13:16-17). Those who try to oppose him will face trouble in the Tribulation so great that unless God shortened the days no one would survive (Matt. 24:21-22).

Christ's Return

The coming of Christ will bring the rule of Antichrist to an end. It is the great event to which all Scripture looks forward. The Old Testament prophets spoke of it, though the first and second comings often merged in their thinking. Jesus Himself frequently referred to it: "I will come back and take you to be with Me that you also may be where I am" (John 14:3); and, "Immediately after the distress of those days . . . the sign of the Son of Man will appear in the sky. . . . . They will see the Son of Man coming on the clouds of the sky, with power and great glory" (Matt. 24:29-30). As the disciples watched Jesus' ascension, "two men dressed in white stood beside them. 'Men of Galilee,' they said, 'why do you stand here looking into the sky? This same Jesus, who has been taken from you into heaven, will come back in the same way you have seen Him go into heaven' " (Acts 1:10-11). Paul also emphasizes it: "For the Lord Himself will come down from heaven, with a loud command, with the voice of the archangel and with the trumpet call of God, and the dead in Christ will rise first" (1 Thes. 4:16).

The second coming of Christ is the great expectation of the church. As Christians we should, with Paul, love to look for that "blessed hope [and] the glorious appearing of our great God and our Saviour Jesus Christ" (Titus 2:13). His coming is an incentive for holy living: "And now, dear children, continue in Him, so that when He appears we may be confident and unashamed before Him at His coming"; and, "Everyone who has this hope in Him purifies himself, just as He is pure" (1 John 2:28; 3:3).

Views of the Rapture

Bible scholars are not completely agreed as to whether the Second Coming is a single event or has two phases. Many evangelicals distinguish between Christ's coming *for* His saints in the Rapture and His coming *with* His saints in the revelation of His power.

Among premillennialists (who believe Christ will return *before* He reigns with His resurrected saints for a thousand years), there are three views, commonly known as the pre-, mid-, and posttribulation views of the Rapture.

Those who hold the pretribulation view believe that Christ

will return *for* His church *before* the Great Tribulation, which, therefore, believers will not have to endure. After this period of turmoil and affliction on earth, Christ will return again *with* His church. He will rule as King during the Millennium. The Tribulation, it is believed, coincides with the seventieth "week" mentioned in Daniel's prophecy: "And he [the prince that is to come, or Antichrist] shall confirm the covenant with many [i.e., with Israel] for one week; and in the midst of the week he shall cause the sacrifice and the oblation [in the temple at Jerusalem] to cease, and for the overspreading of abomination he shall make it desolate, even until the consummation . . . shall be poured upon the desolate" (Dan. 9:27; cf. v. 26, KJV).

By comparing the whole prophecy (Dan. 9) with parallel passages, it appears these "weeks" are "sevens" of *years*, not *days*. According to pretribulation interpretation, therefore, the Tribulation will be a literal seven-year period, ruled by Antichrist, just before his final defeat by Christ. Emphasis is laid in the pretribulation Rapture view, though Christians are not strangers to suffering, on the fact that the final Great Tribulation will not involve believers and will be unique in its awfulness (Matt. 24:21).

The midtribulation view holds that the Rapture will take place in the *middle* of the seventieth "week," three and a half years after its beginning. The posttribulation view is held by premillenarians who believe that Christ's rapture (coming *for* His saints) and His revelation (coming *with* His saints) are one and the same event, occurring just *after* the Tribulation and just before the Millennium.

Is anything yet to happen before Christ can return for His own? Those holding the pretribulation view feel there is nothing to prevent the Rapture from happening at "any moment." This "perhaps today" awareness encourages many Christians to live each day in the light of their Lord's imminent return. Most of those having mid- or posttribulation convictions believe, of course, that certain events (primarily the Tribulation, or the first half of it) must take place before Christ comes again to earth.

The Millennium

Another related and important question has to do with whether or not the Millennium is literal. Premillenarians believe that Christ will have a literal thousand-year reign: "I saw thrones on which were seated those who had been given authority to judge. And I saw the souls of those who had been beheaded because of their testimony for Jesus and because of the Word of God. They had not worshiped the beast or his image and had not received his mark on their foreheads or their hands. They came to life and reigned with Christ a thousand years" (Rev. 20:4). This reign will follow the binding and imprisoning of Satan (20:1-3) so that he may no longer deceive the nations.

Some view the Millennium as an extension and visible expression of Christ's reign in the hearts of His people on earth and in heaven. Others see it as a fulfillment of God's promises to Israel, involving the restoration of the Jews to their homeland as a nation and the reestablishment of a literal throne, king, temple, and sacrificial system.

Many Bible scholars feel that the idea of a literal Millennium cannot be harmonized with biblical eschatology (teaching about the last days). They view the Millennium as a symbol of the ideal church, and therefore are called "amillennialists."

Still another amillenarian view says that the symbolic language of The Revelation represents God's working in history, and that the kingdom of God is to be realized through the preaching of the Gospel. The missionary task of the church, they claim, includes the ultimate Christianizing of society.[2]

Jesus Is Coming!

Whatever points of view expositors take on the Tribulation, the Rapture, and the Millennium, it is thrilling to realize that all agree on the great, glorious, and incontestable fact that *Jesus is coming again.* The details of His next appearance are interesting and important to study, but differences in interpretation should never obscure the fact itself.

It is significant that neither our Lord nor the prophets and apostles mention the return of Christ for speculative purposes, but always as a motive for practical daily holiness. We could summarize the doctrine: "Since everything will be destroyed . . . what kind of people ought you to be? You ought to live holy and godly lives" (2 Peter 3:11).

Two Resurrections

Some momentous events will take place at the coming of Christ. The resurrection of the believing dead will then occur, and we who are still alive will be glorified (1 Cor. 15:52) and caught up "to meet the Lord in the air" (1 Thes. 4:17). The resurrection of the dead is emphasized in the New Testament, but it is taught throughout Scripture. Even Job said, "I know that my Redeemer lives, and that in the end He will stand upon the earth. And after my skin has been destroyed, yet in my flesh I will see God; I myself will see Him with my own eyes—I, and not another" (Job 19:25-27).

David anticipated this resurrection (Ps. 16:9) and Daniel mentioned it (Dan. 12:1-3). Jesus taught it repeatedly and emphasized that it will include *all* people: "A time is coming when all who are in their graves will hear His voice and come out—those who have done good will rise to live, and those who have done evil will rise to be condemned (John 5:28-29).

That the resurrection is a physical rather than a merely spiritual event is proved by the resurrection of Lazarus (John 11:44) and by that of our Lord Himself (Luke 24:39).

The resurrection of the body is part of our total redemption (Rom. 8:23). A Christian should not long to be delivered from the body, with all of its weaknesses and problems, but for the body's redemption. "For while we are in this tent, we groan and are burdened, because we do not wish to be unclothed but to be clothed with our heavenly dwelling, so that what is mortal may be swallowed up by life" (2 Cor. 5:4). Our resurrection bodies will not be identical with the ones we have now, but will be closely related to them.

Believers will be resurrected at the coming of Christ (1 Thes. 4:16). This will be the first resurrection (cf. John 5:28-29), of which Paul wanted to be part (Phil. 3:11). It is, literally, the resurrection "out of the dead." That is, the righteous will be raised from among the wicked.

There is clearly a time lapse between the resurrection of believers to glory and the resurrection of unbelievers to judgment. Though we cannot be dogmatic as to the *exact* length of this interval, *at least a thousand years* will separate the two resurrections: "I saw the souls of those who had been beheaded because of their testimony for Jesus and because of the word of God. They had not worshiped the beast or his image and had not received his mark on their foreheads or their hands. They came to life and reigned with Christ a thousand years. (The rest of the dead did not come to life until the thousand years were ended.) This is the first resurrection. Blessed and holy are those who have part in the first resurrection. The second death has no power over them, but they will be priests of God and of Christ and will reign with Him for a thousand years" (Rev. 20:4-6).

The Dead

What about the condition of the dead before they are resurrected? The Scriptures affirm the conscious existence of both the wicked and the righteous after death and before their resurrections, but give few details. It seems clear that the soul is without a body and that believers are in a condition of conscious joy. Unbelievers, however, await the resurrection in a state of suffering (Luke 16:23). Paul was willing "to be away from the body and at home with the Lord" (2 Cor. 5:8). He said, referring to death, that he preferred "to depart and to be with Christ, which is better by far" (Phil. 1:23). Dead believers are at rest: "Blessed are the dead who die in the Lord from now on. . . . They will rest from their labor" (Rev. 14:13).

Death is frequently described in the Bible as sleep. In the Old Testament the term *sleep* is applied to *all* the dead, but in the New Testament it applies mostly to the *righteous* dead. Paul used the word only of believers. This term does not apply to the soul or spirit; it does not imply total unconsciousness until the resurrection. It rather implies unconsciousness with reference to *earthly life*, for which consciousness the body is necessary. The dead are "asleep" so far as this world is concerned, but this in no way implies that they are asleep or unconscious to the other world or that their spirits are totally unconscious.

"Soul-sleep" is nowhere taught in Scripture. Passages quoted to prove this doctrine refer primarily to bodily or physical life. All that we have said about the state of the righteous dead bears this out.

The consciousness of the unrighteous dead is also clearly taught. They are in prison (1 Peter 3:19), which would be unnecessary if they were unconscious. The story of the rich man and Lazarus (Luke 16:19-31), whatever else it may or may not teach, shows that the unrighteous dead experience conscious suffering and punishment.

No Purgatory

The passages cited clearly refute the doctrine of purgatory. A person dies either as one who has been redeemed or as one who is under judgment. After death there is no passing over from one condition to the other. Final judgment or redemption simply settles what has already begun at the time of death.

More is said about the condition of the dead than about their location. In the Old Testament the souls of all the dead are spoken of as going to *sheol*, which is translated *grave, hell*, or *pit*. "You will not abandon me to the grave, nor will You let Your Holy One see decay" (Ps. 16:10). Sheol is a place of sorrow. "The snares of death confronted me" (2 Sam. 22:6), said David. *Hades*, translated *hell* and *grave*, is the New Testament equivalent of sheol. Other New Testament terms for the intermediate state include *paradise* (Luke 23:43) and *Abraham's bosom* (16:22).

The Judgments

But the intermediate state will be succeeded at last by the final judgment, toward which all history is heading. God is the Ruler of all men, the Lawgiver, and the final Judge. Sometimes

131

the Bible mentions God (the Father) as judge: "God, the judge of all" (Heb. 12:23); and sometimes it mentions Christ: "The Lord Jesus Christ . . . shall judge the quick and the dead at His appearing and His kingdom" (2 Tim. 4:1, KJV). The relationship of the Father and the Son in judgment is made clear: "He [God, the Father] has set a day when He will judge the world with justice by the Man [Christ] He has appointed. He has given proof of this to all men by raising Him from the dead" (Acts 17:31).

God is judging men and nations continually, but there will be a final judgment which all previous judgments foreshadow. It will be an extension of past and present judgment. An unbeliever "stands *condemned* already, because he has not believed in the name of God's one and only Son" (John 3:18, italics added). A believer, on the other hand, "*has* [present tense] eternal life, and will not be condemned; he has crossed over from death to life" (John 5:24, italics added).

The purpose of final judgment will not be to *ascertain* the quality of an individual's character, but to *disclose* his character and to assign him to the eternal place corresponding to what he is because of his trust or lack of trust in God.

Several future judgments are mentioned in Scripture. The judgment of the living nations (Matt. 25:31-46), according to premillennialists, will take place at the return of Christ with His saints. It will lead to the setting up of the millennial kingdom.

Believers will be judged, but not with unbelievers: "We must all appear before the Judgment Seat of Christ, that each one may receive what is due him for the things done while in the body, whether good or bad" (2 Cor. 5:10). It is clear that this judgment does not decide a believer's salvation, but appraises his works. A Christian, in this judgment, can suffer loss of reward. "This is a judgment, not for destiny, but for adjustment, for reward or loss, according to our works, for position in the kingdom: every man according as his work shall be," writes William Evans.[3]

The final judgment of the unsaved will be at the great white throne of God. John describes it:

"I saw a great white throne, and Him who was seated on it. Earth and sky fled from His presence, and there was no place for them. And I saw the dead, great and small, standing before the throne, and books were opened. Another book was opened, which is the Book of Life. The dead were judged according to what they had done as recorded in the books. The sea gave up the dead that were in it, and death and Hades gave up the dead that were in them, and each person was judged according to what he had done. Then death and Hades were thrown in the lake of fire. The lake of fire is the second death. If anyone's name was not found written in the Book of Life, he was thrown into the fire" (Rev. 20:11-15).

The final judgment of Satan will occur just before that of the Great White Throne: "The devil, who deceived them [men], was thrown into the lake of burning sulfur" (Rev. 20:10). Presumably Satan's angels will be judged at the same time, for Jesus spoke of "eternal fire prepared for the devil *and his angels*" (Matt. 25:41, italics added).

Hell

The final destiny of the wicked is hell. This awesome place is described in various ways. It is a place or state of unquenchable (Mark 9:43) and everlasting (Matt. 25:41) fire. It is spoken of as a lake of fire and brimstone (Rev. 20:10). That figurative language is used in these descriptions may be indicated by the fact that death and hell will be cast into it.

Hell is conceived of as outer darkness (Matt. 8:12). It is described as a place of eternal torment and punishment (Rev. 14:10-11). If figurative language is involved, it is obviously symbolic of something so awful no one in his right mind could be indifferent to avoiding it. Strong describes hell as "the loss of all good, whether physical or spiritual, and the misery of an evil conscience banished from God and the society of the holy and dwelling under God's positive curse forever."[4]

Nowhere in Scripture is there any trace of the idea that hell is a kind of "Jolly Boys' Club," absence from which would cause us to miss our friends. This flippant notion is Satan's lie. Hell is "the blackness of darkness forever" (Jude 13, KJV)— utter aloneness. C.S. Lewis defined hell as "nothing but yourself for all eternity"! This is not the whole truth about hell, but it describes one of its most awful aspects.

The future punishment of the wicked is not annihilation. Vos Geerhardus states:

> In support of the doctrine of conditional immortality [that the lost ultimately cease to exist] it has been urged that other terms descriptive of the fate of the condemned, such as "perdition," "corruption," "destruction," and "death" point to a cessation of being. This, however, rests on an unscriptural interpretation of these terms, which everywhere in the Old and New Testaments designate a state of existence with an undesirable content—never the pure negation of existence—just as "life" in Scripture describes a positive mode of being, never mere existence as such. Perdition, corruption, destruction, and death [refer to] the welfare of the ethical, spiritual character of man, without implying the annihilation of his physical existence."[5]

There is no biblical evidence for believing in the final restoration of the lost or in the universal salvation of all men. Perhaps the clearest disproof of these notions, as well as of final annihilation, is the fact that *the same word* is used to describe both punishment and life: "Then they will go away to *eternal* punishment, but the righteous to *eternal* life" (Matt. 25:46). However we may try to qualify the word so that it means "agelong" rather than "everlasting," we must apply the same qualification to the destinies of the righteous and the wicked. We cannot, consistently, deny eternal punishment without also denying eternal life. And "eternal life" is *everlasting* life. *Eternal* certainly means "everlasting" when it is applied to God. Why should it mean anything else when it modifies "punishment"?

There are, however, *degrees* of punishment in hell and of

reward in heaven. Some, at the Judgment Seat of Christ in heaven, will suffer loss of reward because their works of "wood, hay, or straw" will not stand the test of fire (1 Cor. 3:12-15). Their capacity for enjoyment, though unlimited in duration, will be less than that of others. Similarly, the wicked will be judged, "every man according to his works" (Rev. 20:13, KJV). "The servant who knows his master's will and does not get ready or does not do what his master wants will be beaten with many blows. But the one who does not know and does things deserving punishment will be beaten with few blows" (Luke 12:47-48).

God, in His love, has done everything necessary to deliver men from eternal punishment. His justice requires that He punish sin, but His love provides salvation freely for all who will accept it. Those in hell are there because they refused or ignored God's love; they are solely responsible for their condition. The realization of this truth will surely be one of the most painful experiences of perdition.

Heaven

The final destiny of the righteous is heaven. Heaven is most simply defined as where God is. It is a place of rest (Heb. 4:9), of glory (2 Cor. 4:17), of holiness (Rev. 21:27), of worship (Rev. 19:1), of fellowship with others (Heb. 12:23), and of being with God (Rev. 21:3). "He will wipe every tear from their eyes. There will be no more death or mourning or crying or pain, for the old order of things has passed away" (Rev. 21:4).

Believers may receive one or more crowns—the crown of life (James 1:12), the crown of glory (1 Peter 5:4), and the crown of righteousness (2 Tim. 4:8). Those who have been won for Christ through our witness become our crown of rejoicing (1 Thes. 2:19).

Everything in heaven will be new: "The earth and everything in it will be laid bare . . . but we are looking forward to a new heaven and a new earth, the home of righteousness" (2 Peter 3:10, 13). John reports that he "saw a new heaven and a new earth, for the first heaven and the first earth had passed away, and there was no longer any sea. I saw the Holy City, the new Jerusalem, coming down out of heaven from God. . . . And they will reign for ever and ever" (Rev. 21:1-2; 22:5).

God's kingdom will be established when all things are put under His feet. Then, "at the name of Jesus every knee [shall] bow . . . and every tongue confess that Jesus Christ is Lord, to the glory of God the Father" (Phil. 2:10-11). The kingdoms of this world shall be the kingdoms of our Lord, and He shall reign forever and ever. His will will be done on earth as it is done in heaven.

Heaven will not be the boring experience of strumming a harp on a cloud, as some facetiously characterize it. It will be the most dynamic, expanding, exhilarating experience conceivable. Our problem now is that, with our finite minds, we cannot imagine it.

When we've been there ten thousand years,
    Bright shining as the sun,
We've no less days to sing His praise,
    Than when we first begun.

JOHN NEWTON

N O T E S

Chapter 1

[1]B.B. Warfield, *The Inspiration and Authority of the Bible* (New York: Oxford University Press, 1927), p. 299.
[2]T.C. Hammond, *In Understanding Be Men* (Downers Grove, Ill.: InterVarsity Press, 1968), p. 13.
[3]J.N. Birdsell, "Canon of the New Testament," in *New Bible Dictionary (NBD)* (Grand Rapids: Wm. B. Eerdmans Publishing Co., 1962), p. 194.
[4]A.R. Millard, *Treasures from Bible Times* (Tring, Belleville, Sydney, "A Lion Book," 1985), p. 14.

Chapter 2

[1]A.H. Strong, *Systematic Theology* (Philadelphia: Judson Press, 1907), p. 255.
[2]Hammond, *In Understanding,* p. 44.
[3]R.A. Finlayson, "Holiness," *NBD,* p. 530.
[4]Ibid., p. 530.
[5]R.A. Finlayson, "Trinity," *NBD,* p. 1298.
[6]Ibid., p. 1298.
[7]Ibid., p. 1300.
[8]Hammond, *In Understanding,* p. 54.

[9]Finlayson, "Trinity," *NBD*, p. 1300.
[10]Hammond, *In Understanding*, p. 66.
[11]Ibid., p. 56.
[12]J.I. Packer, *Evangelism and the Sovereignty of God* (Downers Grove, Ill.: InterVarsity Press, 1961), pp. 18-19.

Chapter 3

[1]Strong, *Theology*, p. 676.
[2]Ibid., p. 673.
[3]Hammond, *In Understanding*, p. 101.
[4]R.A. Finlayson, *The Story of Theology* (Downers Grove, Ill.: InterVarsity Press, 1963), pp. 24-25.

Chapter 4

[1]Leon Morris, "Atonement," *NBD*, p. 108.
[2]Leon Morris, "Propitiation," *NBD*, p. 1046.
[3]Strong, *Theology*, p. 740.
[4]Finlayson, *Theology*, p. 38.
[5]Strong, *Theology*, p. 766.
[6]James Denney, *The Death of Christ* (Downers Grove, Ill.: InterVarsity Press, 1964), p. 3.
[7]Hammond, *In Understanding*, p. 122.
[8]Robert J. Little, *Here's Your Answer* (Chicago: Moody Press, 1967), p. 206.

Chapter 5

[1]Hammond, *In Understanding*, p. 71.
[2]D.M. Edwards, "Image," in *International Standard Bible Encyclopedia (ISBE)* (Grand Rapids: Wm. B. Eerdmans Publishing Co., 1939), p. 1450.
[3]R.J. Wallace, "Man," *NBD*, p. 777.
[4]Hammond, *In Understanding*, p. 77.
[5]John Murray, "Sin," *NBD*, p. 1190.

Chapter 6

[1]G.W. Walters, "Holy Spirit," *NBD*, p. 531f.

Notes

[2]E.Y. Mullins, "Holy Spirit," *ISBE*, p. 1409.
[3]Strong, *Theology*, p. 342.
[4]Hammond, *In Understanding*, p. 131.

Chapter 7

[1]D.W.B. Robinson, "Church," *NBD*, pp. 228-229.
[2]Strong, *Theology*, p. 887.
[3]Ibid., p. 890.
[4]Leon Morris, *Ministers of God* (Downers Grove, Ill.: InterVarsity Press, 1969), p. 91.
[5]Hammond, *In Understanding*, p. 162ff.
[6]Morris, *Ministers of God*, p. 92ff.
[7]John Dall, *Encyclopedia of Religion and Ethics* (Edinburgh: T. & T. Clark, 1918), p. 264.

Chapter 8

[1]Little, *Here's Your Answer*, p. 192.

Chapter 9

[1]Leon Morris, "Faith," *NBD*, p. 413.
[2]Strong, *Theology*, p. 809.
[3]J.I. Packer, "Election," *NBD*, p. 360.
[4]Charles Simeon, *Expository Outlines on the Whole Bible* (Grand Rapids: Zondervan, reprint 1956), vol. I, xvii-xviii.

Chapter 10

[1]Helmut Thielicke, *The Waiting Father* (New York: Harper, 1959).
[2]George E. Ladd, "Eschatology," *NBD*, p. 390.
[3]Wm. Evans, *The Great Doctrines of the Bible* (Chicago: Moody Press, 1949), p. 254.
[4]Strong, *Theology*, p. 1034.
[5]Geerhardus Vos, "Eschatology of the New Testament," *ISBE*, p. 991.